A Camping Cookbook

by

Josh Sutton

Guyrope Gourmet
Published in the UK in 2013 by
Punk Publishing Ltd, 3 The Yard, Pegasus Place, London SE11 5SD
www.punkpublishing.co.uk

A catalogue record of this book is available from the
British Library.

ISBN 978-1-906889-60-9

10 8 6 4 2 1 3 5 7 9

INVERCLYDE LIBRARIES

For Anne-Marie,
my original Good Companion

Contents

Introduction

I LOVE FOOD. I love eating it, I love looking at it, I love writing about it but, most of all, I love preparing and cooking it for my family and friends. I love camping, too, having spent most of my holidays under canvas since I was a kid. Being the Guyrope Gourmet lets me marry those passions. Fuelled by a fierce desire to do better than bangers and beans, I like to add a little adventure to the campsite kitchen, to try something different, and to have a lot of fun. Using the recipes in this book, anyone can be a Guyrope Gourmet, quickly throwing a delicious meal together with barely any faff.

How I became the Guyrope Gourmet is a story steeped in romance. I like to think that my culinary camping skills played a key role in courting the woman who later became my wife. Soon after meeting, at the tail end of the twentieth century, we set off on a camping adventure. As I showed off with my lamb stew and my stuffed trout, I rather thought I was making an impression. And the fact that she later accepted my marriage proposal – offered on a campsite, after a fine supper of fresh grilled fish – only went to prove it. The seeds of an idea were sown. Dishes that pack a fancy punch but are actually deliciously simple – gourmet food that can be cooked and eaten outdoors, under the stars – well, I mused, there might be mileage in that. Talking with friends and fellow campers, it seemed I was right: many people were yearning for inspiration in the camp kitchen.

The name sprang out of nowhere while I was sitting on a train in Birmingham New Street station. I was already cooking fine food in the camp kitchen, so I asked a friend to build a website (www.guyropegourmet.com) where I could display a few of my recipes. I was amazed by the great feedback I got. Before I knew it, I was pitched at a food festival, entertaining a hundred people by cooking paella and messing around on my ukulele. It went down well, everyone got to taste the food – and some came back for seconds!

Camping has been a part of my life since early childhood. I remember the thrill, on family holidays, of helping my father pitch the Black's Good Companion tent. The familiar, musty smell of the orange cotton flysheet and the sheen of the waterproof groundsheet heralded the start of each new adventure. But then came the food. The dull, unadventurous food. Baked beans, tinned tomato soup and Mother's Pride sliced white bread slathered in Stork margarine. Even as a child, I longed for something more... *exciting.*

I learned my own cooking skills on the hop, and continue to do so. Memories of my grandfather's delicious pearl barley-filled soups, my mother teaching me to make Tatws Pum Munud (you can read all about that later) and the disappointed look on Mrs Walker's face when I chose to cook egg and chips for my home economics CSE exam, are all I can claim by way of a culinary heritage. A little later, my step-mum, Jude, taught me to balance flavours and to cook by taste. Once I'd flown the nest, my backpacking days opened my eyes to different styles of cooking and how to always make the best of what's available. Slowly and surely I honed my craft under canvas, gathering tips and ideas with each new camping adventure.

More than ninety recipes are set out in the following pages. All were conjured up at some point on a campsite, and all are

dishes that I cook regularly when I go camping with my family. They've been invented, begged, borrowed, stolen and adapted from all over the place, and I've done my best to ensure that credit is given where credit is due throughout.

Of course a good meal – especially a Guyrope Gourmet meal – deserves a good wine, or even a good local ale, so I've also offered a drink suggestion with most recipes. I'm deeply indebted to my friend and wine aficionado, James Stark, who provided many of the wine ideas. His suggestions are just that – an opportunity to try something new, perhaps, and to have a bit of fun.

And fun, of course, is the key. I'm no purist – far from it. The realities of camping or cooking outdoors will often determine what sort of meal you end up eating. When the rain won't let up and the kids won't settle, the last thing you'll want is to be shelling peas. And there's no need to be precious about this book, either. The Guyrope Gourmet cookbook is designed to be used and abused. Don't worry about spilling olive oil on page 13 or smearing tomato puree across your favourite recipe. That's supposed to happen; it means you're getting value for money. It's meant to be a practical book, so make notes in the margins, use it as an impromptu placemat, or wave it around to fan the flames of the barbecue. The main thing is to use it to get out there, get to it, and above all, enjoy yourself!

Local interest

One of the best things about cooking and eating well while camping is that you're more or less obliged to use fresh and often local ingredients. While many campers are tempted down the path of least resistance – a path lined with processed and tinned goods – using local ingredients adds excitement, adventure and, above all, flavour to a dish. Baby carrots still coated with soil, or lettuce so fresh that the outer leaves have yet to wilt, will always out-perform their machine-washed and vacuum-packed mass-produced counterparts. Camping in Britain offers an inroad to a fantastic range of local produce. If you're pitched high in the Wye Valley, doesn't it make sense to use a couple of prime Welsh lamb neck fillets to rustle up a tasty stew? And who could resist a fresh lobster feast while camping on the Norfolk coast? You can even find locally made chorizo in the Yorkshire Dales!

The slow food movement has really taken off in Britain. Farmers and specialist producers have made great strides in promoting local food, and barely a month goes by without a food festival being held somewhere. Year-round, meanwhile, farmers' markets bring locally produced food to within a few miles of most people's doorsteps – or, should I say, tent flaps. What's more, many campsites in Britain have their own farm shops and sell local produce on site.

Of course, there's always a chance that local produce may just be beyond reach. Perhaps you showed up on the Wednesday while the organic food fair took place on the previous Monday, or it was raining so hard that a trip to the farmers' market didn't seem viable. It could well be that the only "local produce" available is limited to the shelves of the village corner shop or convenience store. This doesn't mean that you have to revert to bangers and beans. In fact, shopping at the local convenience store makes a positive contribution to the local economy. While it may be lacking in the fresh food department (though evidence has often proved otherwise), it's often capable of coming up trumps. Have a look around, see what's available and get stuck in.

Kit and caboodle

Clearly, there's only so much you can cram into the back of a Ford Focus estate, but as far as I'm concerned, you can never have too much kit. Reliable, good-quality equipment is a prerequisite for cooking in the field. It is for *all* cooking, really, but even more so while you're camping, when there are no kitchen cupboards to raid if your best-laid plans go belly-up. This section is about setting out your stall. Use it, if you like, as an excuse to nip out and buy a couple of new gadgets. (I'm a sucker for gadgets.)

The cooker

Pack a two-ring cooker plus grill (the grill makes all the difference), and the world's your oyster. Though my early dalliances with campsite cooking were on a Trangia stove — an amazing piece of kit and an aluminium icon of Scandinavian design — nowadays I cook on an Outwell Chef Cooker Deluxe, which has two hobs and a grill. It's good at what it does and is easy to use (and to keep clean).

I use the large blue Camping Gaz "R907" bottles with my stove; many campsites sell them. A full bottle will burn for about seven hours. They're quite pricey — but a large chunk of cash is a deposit on the bottle itself, and refills aren't too expensive. And here's a handy tip offered by someone in the audience at a Guyrope Gourmet cookery demonstration: you can often find empty bottles at your local waste-recycling yard. Clear it with the staff and you should be able to take one for free.

The coolbox

Good, efficient cool storage is essential. Best, of course, is an electric coolbox which, whether it's powered by the cigarette lighter in your vehicle (take care not to flatten the battery!) or by the hook-up at the campsite, will offer refrigeration for your whole trip. Failing that, a good-quality, well-insulated coolbox with four or five ice packs will keep most things fresh for a couple of days. It needs to be rigid, with walls at least 3cm thick and a capacity of at least 30 litres — one of those floppy things from the supermarket just won't do. The more densely packed the coolbox, the more efficient it will be, and the more you open it the sooner it's going to warm up. Spend a moment or two thinking about the order in which you pack the thing. Stuff that's going to be used pretty quickly needs to be on the top. Bags of frozen food can assist the ice packs in doing their job, but be sure to use them up in a timely fashion. Frozen tiger prawns are not going to stay frozen for a whole weekend!

The Spin Cycle 1600 rpm barbecue

I'd recommend bringing a portable barbecue. They're great for cooking fish and burgers and for chargrilling vegetables. And this little beauty – an old washing machine drum – is particularly clever, doubling as a fire pit (I've only once come across a campsite owner who wasn't happy to let me use it as a fire after cooking). I picked up mine from a washing machine repair shop for about £20, attached three old tent poles as legs to raise it up off the grass, and added an oven shelf over the top to act as a grill. Once the cooking's done, simply throw in a dry log or two and – hey presto – the barbecue becomes a fire pit. Brilliant for toasting marshmallows – and, with the flames peeping through the holes in the side, an atmospheric focus for post-prandial ghost stories.

The 1600 rpm does, however, take up quite a bit of room in the car. You may prefer to pack a more portable version – there are lots on the market. For fuel, it's best to use lump-wood charcoal, which burns better than briquettes and makes less mess.

Tempting though it is to throw the food on as soon as possible, make sure you wait until the coals turn grey; a dancing flame will blacken your sardines with foul-tasting soot in a matter of minutes. And finally, at the risk of sounding like my old home economics teacher (a risk worth taking) remember that burning charcoal gives off carbon monoxide – an odourless, poisonous gas. Never bring the barbecue into your tent.

On the subject of fires, most campers dream of an open fire to cook on. Sadly, though, and for all manner of reasons, these tend not to be allowed on campsites nowadays. If you're lucky enough to be staying on a site that does permit them, or are building an impromptu fire on a beach, then remember that food cooks best over embers. Never leave a fire unattended and always douse it with water before hitting the sack.

Pots and pans (and bits and pieces)

A decent non-stick frying pan will prove invaluable; it will save elbow grease when it comes to the washing up. You have to look after non-stick pans, though. There's no point in shelling out good money for a quality piece of kit and then going at it hell for leather with a steel pan scourer, and you need to use wooden or plastic implements to make sure the Teflon stays on. Other useful bits of kit:

- Two saucepans, 15cm & 20cm (with lids)
- Large stockpot (with lid)
- A wok & lid (not essential – but if you have one you might as well bring it along)
- Wooden chopping board
- Set of three sharp knives (one large, one medium and one little 'un)

- Grater
- Pestle & mortar
- Camping kettle (water boils more quickly in a kettle – which saves gas)
- Tupperware boxes (handy for storing chopped and grated ingredients and leftovers)
- Kitchen paper
- Measuring jug
- Wooden spoons & spatulas
- Tea towels
- Mixing bowl

Basics for the camping larder

Most of the condiments used in this book come in a jar or a tin and will last a while without spoiling, so it won't hurt to bring along a plentiful supply. I'm clearly not providing a definitive list here – it could go on forever! Remember that even if you've forgotten something, you can probably get it – or something good enough – nearby.

- Olive oil (what would we do without it?)
- Flaked sea salt (it may sound precious, but it really does make a difference!)
- Pepper mill (and plenty of black peppercorns)
- Cumin, coriander and fennel seeds (whole)
- Paprika
- Dried chillies
- Fresh herbs: rosemary, thyme, coriander, basil, bay leaves
- Garlic

The camping box

Another idea is to keep most of your essential camping gear in one camping box. You can pick up a large plastic container (mine has wheels) from any DIY superstore. It makes packing the car less arduous, and means you don't have to rethink the packing list every time.

Next time…

One of the best packing tips I have ever received was from a bunch of Aussies that I had the fortune to camp with many years ago. As soon as you've set up camp (and cracked open a beer, obviously), the first thing you should do is to make a list of what you forgot to bring. That way, your next trip will always be better than your last. Simple.

Breakfasts

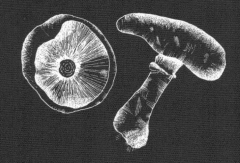

MANY OF US CHOOSE to eat the same thing for breakfast every day. There's not often much time before the school run or the dash to work, so we grab what's easy and what we know. When you're camping, though, things slow down a little, offering the perfect opportunity to try something different. Of the recipes I've chosen here, all of which are easily put together on a campsite, the scrambled eggs with smoked salmon probably remains, to this day, my favourite camping breakfast. For me, it's the very taste of a sunny summer morning in the British countryside.

Breakfast pancakes

A good few years back I was travelling across the States with some pals. We'd stayed overnight on a campsite near Memphis. As we were driving off in the morning, a peculiar sound came from under the bonnet (or should that be hood?) of our car. Within seconds, the chap from the trailer next to us appeared offering to help. "I'm a mechanic," he said. "My wife will fix y'all some pancakes while I adjust your power-steering belt!" The car was mended in about fifteen minutes, but we stayed for a good couple of hours, chatting with these friendly strangers over breakfast and jugs of coffee. To this day, breakfast pancakes always remind me of their kindness.

Place the flour, baking powder, salt and sugar in a mixing bowl. Pour over the eggs and the softened butter and beat the mixture together.

Add the milk a little at a time, stirring with a wooden spoon; this will help prevent a lumpy batter. The batter should be the consistency of double cream when mixed.

Melt a knob of butter in a non-stick frying pan and, using a ladle, pour in a dollop of batter mix. Fry over a moderate heat until bubbles appear, then flip and cook the other side for a couple of minutes.

Serve with maple syrup or a squeeze of lemon.

Ingredients Serves 4
(makes about 8 pancakes)

- ○ 225g plain flour
- ○ 1 heaped tsp baking powder
- ○ A pinch of salt
- ○ 1 tsp sugar
- ○ 2 large eggs
- ○ 30g butter, softened
- ○ 300ml milk
- ○ Butter for frying
- ○ Maple syrup or lemon

Equipment
Mixing bowl, wooden spoon, non-stick frying pan, ladle

Eggs in a mess

Ingredients Serves 1

- 1 slice of bread
- Olive oil
- 1 egg
- Fresh ground black pepper

Equipment

Non-stick frying pan (essential if you want to avoid tears!), wooden spatula

I owe this recipe to one of the early pioneers of children's Saturday morning TV programmes, *Why Don't You (Just Switch Off Your Television Set and Go and Do Something Less Boring Instead?)*. My brother and I thought we were smart beyond belief when, in response to the "switch off your television" bit we'd yell at the screen, "because if we did, we wouldn't be able to watch Why Don't You!"

Anyway, this dish was actually called "eggs in a nest" by the blonde kid that cooked it on the programme. It was renamed by my uncle after, at the age of ten, I attempted to recreate it on holiday in Greece. I gloriously messed up. The egg stuck to the pan and I promptly burst into tears!

It's a big favourite in our camp to this day – and especially with my kids when I pretend to cry while making it.

Gently poke a hole, about the size of an egg yolk, in the slice of bread.

Pour a glug of olive oil into a non-stick frying pan and place over a moderate heat. Put the slice of bread into the pan and crack the egg into the hole in the bread. The white will spill over a bit, but it's supposed to.

Cook the bread and egg for a minute or two and then flip it using a wooden spatula.

Cook the other side for a minute or two – no longer than that, though, or there may be tears (and a solid yolk).

Season with black pepper and serve immediately.

Scrambled eggs and smoked salmon

Ingredients Serves 4

- 4 eggs
- Sea salt & fresh ground black pepper
- A dollop of double cream
- A knob of butter
- A small sprig of fresh thyme
- 200g smoked salmon, cut into strips
- Muffins or bagels

Equipment

Mixing bowl/Pyrex jug, non-stick frying pan, wooden spoon, grill

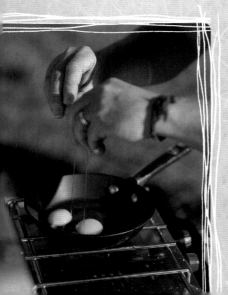

Here's a really simple dish that gives a lift to any start of the day – though for some mysterious reason it seems to work best on a Sunday. It's a classic, as far as I'm concerned, and was one of the dishes that inspired the Guyrope Gourmet idea – a jolly posh breakfast, perfect for eating at camp.

Perfect served on a toasted buttered muffin or bagel.

Crack the eggs into a mixing bowl or Pyrex jug, taking care not to drop any egg-shell fragments into the bowl. Add a pinch of sea salt and black pepper to taste. Beat with a fork until well mixed and add the double cream. Mix again.

Melt a good knob of butter in a non-stick frying pan and throw in the sprig of thyme. Keep the heat low and, using a wooden spoon, turn the thyme through the butter for a minute or two to flavour the butter. Remove the thyme and pour in the egg mixture. Keep on a low heat and stir the eggs as they start to cook.

Just before the eggs are done to your satisfaction, throw in the smoked salmon strips and stir well. Make sure that the salmon goes in right at the last moment – you want it to stay lovely and pink, and overcooking will turn it into a dull, miserable grey.

Alternatively, simply load the eggs onto your bagel or muffin and dress with strips of fresh smoked salmon at that point – no cooking required.

Shakshuka

A hearty breakfast recipe passed on to me by my younger brother – he was taught it first-hand in the highlands of Scotland by a wayward Israeli hitchhiker. I have to say that when Will first described the dish I wasn't convinced, but then I actually cooked it – and here it is!

Shakshuka is popular throughout the Middle East, and though more complicated variations abound, this simple version will take little more than five minutes to make.

It's great served with good chunks of fresh bread.

Heat the olive oil in the non-stick pan and gently fry the sliced onion. When the onion begins to take on some colour, throw in the chopped garlic and the paprika, stir well and cook gently for a couple of minutes.

Add the chopped tomatoes and turn up the heat to reduce the liquid.

When the tomato sauce has reduced by about a third, turn down the heat and crack in the eggs. Cook for a further 5 minutes or until the eggs have turned white.

Season to taste, and garnish with the chopped flat leaf parsley.

Ingredients Serves 2

- A little olive oil
- 1 onion, finely sliced
- 4 cloves of garlic, finely chopped
- 1 tsp paprika
- 1 tin of chopped tomatoes
- 2 eggs
- Sea salt & fresh ground black pepper
- Fresh flat leaf parsley, chopped

Equipment

Sharp knife, non-stick frying pan

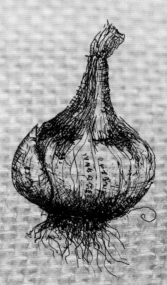

Eggy bread

- 4 eggs
- A splash of milk
- Sea salt & fresh ground black pepper
- 4 slices of bread
- A glug of olive oil
- Maple syrup

Equipment
Mixing jug, shallow bowl, non-stick frying pan

... Or "instant breakfast" by any other name. A substantial start to the day, achieved with barely any effort. Serve hot, with a dollop of maple syrup.

Crack the eggs into a mixing jug, add a splash of milk and a pinch of salt along with a good grind of black pepper. Whisk with a fork and pour into a shallow bowl.

Coat both sides of the sliced bread in the mixture. Warm a glug of olive oil in a non-stick frying pan and fry the eggy bread for 2 or 3 minutes on each side. Done!

Kedgeree

I remember making this in my CSE Home Economics class under the watchful eye of Mrs Walker. I gobbled it all up on the bus home and was given a good telling off from my dad for having eaten what was going to be the family dinner! Rice for breakfast is a throwback to the days of the Raj. It may seem a little on the exotic side, but it really does set you up for the day – and the leftovers make a great lunch.

Put the smoked haddock, peppercorns, saffron and bay leaf into a large saucepan and pour in the milk. Bring to the boil then turn down the heat to a gentle simmer and cook with a lid on for 5 minutes.

Remove the fish from the pan, allow it to cool, and then remove the skin. Strain the remaining milk into a jug and keep.

In a separate pan, melt the butter and cook the chopped onion until it begins to colour. Add the curry powder and the rice and stir in the milk that you've kept from cooking the fish. Add the water and bring to the boil.

As soon as the water boils, turn to a low heat and simmer gently with the lid on for about 10 minutes until the rice has absorbed all of the liquid.

Once the rice is cooked, fork it into a large bowl. Flake the haddock into to rice along with the chopped hard-boiled eggs. Squeeze over the juice of half a lemon, mix it through and add a good handful of chopped fresh flat leaf parsley. Season to taste and serve warm or cold.

Ingredients Serves 4

- 1 fillet of smoked haddock
- 6 black peppercorns
- A small pinch of saffron
- 1 bay leaf
- 285ml milk
- A large knob of butter
- 1 small onion, finely chopped
- 1 tsp curry powder
- 225g basmati rice
- 250ml water
- 4 eggs, hard boiled, peeled and roughly chopped
- Juice of half a lemon
- Fresh flat leaf parsley, chopped
- Sea salt & fresh ground black pepper

Equipment

Two large saucepans with lids, sieve or colander, jug, sharp knife, large bowl

Omelettes

Ingredients
- 2 eggs per person
- Sea salt & fresh ground black pepper
- A drop of milk
- A sprig of fresh thyme (optional)
- A glug of olive oil

Equipment
Pyrex mixing jug, non-stick frying pan

OK, everyone knows you can't make an omelette without breaking eggs. But not everyone knows quite how delicious and sophisticated a well-prepared omelette can be. I often turn to a delightful book by Narcissa Chamberlain, *The Omelette Book*, which features more than three hundred recipes. Among other things, Narcissa warns us not to beat the eggs for too long and not to use a beater – and who am I to ignore her wise words?

Some people like to fold their omelettes – it adds a certain panache! – but serving them flat is probably a little easier.

Crack the eggs into a Pyrex mixing jug or similar. Season and add the eggs and thyme (stripping the leaves from the stalk) and beat thoroughly with a fork.

Heat the olive oil in a decent non-stick frying pan over a moderate heat, pour in the egg mixture and cook for 3 or 4 minutes. You should be able to shake the omelette about in the pan.

You then need to cook the other side. An easy way to flip the omelette is to place an upturned plate over the frying pan, turn the pan over, transfer the omelette onto the plate, and then slide the omelette back into the pan uncooked side down. Cook it for no longer than a minute, and then serve.

To customise this basic dish, gently fry any (or all!) of the following in the pan before adding the beaten eggs:

- Chopped bacon
- Sliced sausages
- Chopped mushrooms
- Thinly sliced (or diced) potatoes
- Sliced chorizo

You could even go mad and add cooked asparagus tips, artichokes, red peppers... the list is practically endless.

"Extra" bacon butties

Ingredients Serves 4
(enough for four butties and an extra spoonful of guacamole for the chef!)

- ○ 2 very ripe avocados (Hass, with the lumpy brown skin, are good)
- ○ 2 spring onions, finely sliced
- ○ Sea salt & fresh ground black pepper
- ○ 4 cherry tomatoes, most of the seeds removed, finely chopped
- ○ A glug of olive oil
- ○ Juice of half a lime
- ○ A small bunch of fresh coriander, chopped
- ○ Good bread (you can toast it f you like)
- ○ Good dry-cured bacon (smoked bacon tastes great with this recipe)

Equipment
Sharp knife, non-stick frying pan

I'll admit to a little subterfuge here – the "extra" refers to a dollop of fine guacamole, but if my kids ever found out that I was putting avocado in their bacon sarnies without letting on all hell would break loose.

My wife, Anne-Marie, brought this recipe back from a trip to New York. It sounded so cosmopolitan that I thought I'd make it in a tent. Kept in a Tupperware box in the coolbox, the guacamole will stay good for a couple of days – the lime juice helps keep it fresh.

For the guacamole, halve the avocados and remove the stones. If they are really ripe, you'll be able to simply squeeze the flesh into a bowl, or scoop it out with a spoon, rather than having to peel and chop them. Add the spring onion, a tiny pinch of salt and a grind of black pepper. Throw in the chopped tomatoes along with a good glug of olive oil and the lime juice.

Mash it all up roughly with a fork and top with a scattering of chopped coriander.

Spread the guacamole evenly over your bread (or toast), build your bacon sandwich and enjoy with a "Noo Yoik" accent.

(I'm not telling you how to make a bacon sandwich!)

Croque Monsieur

This is effectively a cheese and ham toastie in disguise, so you'll need a grill. It's well worth the effort of making the cheesy béchamel sauce to pour over the top – it's the sauce that transforms the humble toastie into something a cut above. And I guarantee that presenting your friends with a bona fide Croque Monsieur on a campsite will see you become the stuff of legend!

Melt the butter in a non-stick frying pan and fry the bread until it begins to brown on one side only. Spread the uncooked side with Dijon mustard and plonk a slice of ham and a good handful of grated cheese on top. Spread the cheese so it covers the ham. Place under the grill and melt the cheese.

Now to the béchamel sauce. In a non-stick saucepan, melt the butter and add the flour. Throw in a little pinch of salt and a grind of black pepper. Mix to a smooth paste with a wooden spoon and cook for a couple of minutes.

Remove from the heat and add the milk a little at a time, stirring well so the sauce doesn't go lumpy. Once all the milk is added, return to the heat and bring to the boil, stirring all the time.

When the sauce begins to thicken, drop in the rest of the grated cheese and stir.

Pour some sauce over the croque and brown the whole thing off under the grill.

Season to taste.

Ingredients Serves 1

For the croque:
- A knob of butter
- 2 slices of good white bread
- Dijon mustard
- A couple of slices of good ham
- About 50g strong cheese, grated – Gruyere or a mature Welsh Teifi cheese would be ideal

For the béchamel sauce:
- 25g butter
- 1 tbsp plain flour
- Sea salt & fresh ground black pepper
- 250ml full-fat milk
- About 50g of the same cheese as used in the sandwich

Equipment

Non-stick frying pan, grater, grill, non-stick saucepan, wooden spoon

The Monty Zoomer

Ingredients (serves 4)

- A glug of olive oil
- 2 cloves of garlic, peeled and finely chopped
- 200g chorizo, skin removed, chopped into 1cm chunks
- 2 large beef tomatoes, roughly chopped (you can use a tin if you don't have fresh to hand)
- Half a red chilli (or a whole chilli if you want extra zoom!), de-seeded and finely chopped
- ½ tsp ground cumin
- 1 tin of kidney beans, drained
- Sea salt & fresh ground black pepper
- 4 eggs
- 4 flour tortillas
- A handful of flat leaf parsley, chopped

Equipment

High sided, non-stick frying pan with lid, a second frying pan, sharp knife, mixing bowl

This pepped-up burrito with a good chilli kick is guaranteed to give your taste buds a quick "zoom" in the morning. It's my Mexican-style take on the good old bangers and beans breakfast, and works well as a brunch, too.

There's a little game going on with the title. I've named this king of breakfasts not only after the mighty Aztec emperor, but also as a way of paying homage to the king-size tent I regularly use for camping holidays with the family – the Outwell Montana, or "Monty" as it is affectionately known. It's a truly huge tent, with room a-plenty; even for those with a penchant for big burritos!

Warm the olive oil in the high-sided frying pan and add the chopped garlic and chorizo. Fry gently for a couple of minutes, until the paprika in the chorizo turns the oil a lovely deep red.

While the chorizo and garlic are cooking, roughly chop the tomatoes.

Add the tomatoes to the frying pan together with the chopped chilli and ground cumin. Give it all a stir, place the lid on the pan, and turn the heat down to low.

Tip the drained kidney beans into a bowl, season well with sea salt and ground black pepper, and mash roughly.

Add the beans to the pan and bring to a gentle simmer for 15 or 20 minutes, keeping the lid on the pan. The tomatoes will start to break down as they cook, and the sauce will thicken. If it gets too dry, add a little water. Take care, though – you don't want it too runny.

Once the sauce is cooked, fry the eggs to your liking in a separate pan.

Spread a good tablespoon of the sauce over a tortilla and place the fried egg on top. Scatter with chopped flat leaf parsley and roll the whole thing up, tucking the edges in as you roll – that's what makes it a burrito, and stops the delicious filling from falling out onto your lap when you take the first bite.

Tapas

TAPA IS THE SPANISH WORD for "lid" or "cover". In the bars of Andalucía it has long been traditional for patrons to offer customers a little snack to go with their drink. I'm not sure I believe the old story that a slice of bread or ham was used as a "lid" to keep the flies out of the glass – I'm more inclined to believe that tapas were a means of keeping a "lid" on the hunger pangs until the evening meal at home. When I first visited Spain in the 1980s, as a wet-behind-the-ears backpacker, many of the bars I stumbled into in Andalucía offered free tapas. Sadly this no longer seems to be the case. More recently, my wife and I spent a long, wonderful evening in a tiny tapas bar in Granada, swooning under a honeyed moon. I was captivated by the young barkeep's enthusiasm for pouring drinks and whipping up amazing food in a matter of moments. He clearly adored his job, and it opened my eyes to a whole new way of eating. I love the idea of making a quick feast of delicious treats for my family and friends – and the twist here, of course, is that I can then dish them all up in a tent!

Bruschetta

Ingredients
This will make about 12 single portions

- French bread, toasted
- A glug of olive oil
- 2 cloves of garlic, finely chopped
- 100g mushrooms, finely chopped
- 8–10 cherry tomatoes, quartered or halved depending on the size
- A sprig of fresh thyme
- Sea salt & fresh ground black pepper

Equipment
Grill (or other means of making toast), non-stick frying pan, sharp knife

Bruschetta works really well when I'm cooking at food festivals. It's so easy to prepare, with just four main ingredients – or five, if you're including the toast – and the bruschetta mix keeps for a while. Freshly picked mushrooms would be great if you can find them – but do make sure you know what you're picking. I generally use the brown chestnut mushrooms, which have lots of good flavour.

When chopping the mushrooms, remember that you'll be serving them on little rounds of toast, so you want the pieces to be fairly small. No one wants to see all this good stuff fall off the toast, stain your shirt and go to waste.

Slice the French bread into rounds for toasting. I always do this first, as the toaster on my camping grill takes a little while to get going. You can prepare the topping while you are toasting the bread.

Warm a little olive oil in a non-stick frying pan, and add the chopped garlic. After a minute, add the chopped mushrooms and stir; the mushrooms will soak up all of the garlicky olive oil. Throw in the tomatoes and the sprig of thyme. Cook gently for about 4 minutes. Add a grind of black pepper and a pinch of salt to taste.

Once the tomatoes have softened, but not totally lost their shape, spoon the mixture onto the toasted bread and serve warm or cold to your liking.

You could drizzle with some really good olive oil if you're feeling extravagant.

Drink suggestion An Italian white like a Verdicchio or a good Soave – or perhaps a light red Bardolino or Valpolicella.

Grilled halloumi with lime

Ingredients Serves 4
- 250g halloumi cheese
- 1 fresh lime
- Fresh ground black pepper

Equipment
Sharp knife, grill

Drink suggestion
A Mexican beer with a wedge of lime in the neck

Something magical happens to halloumi when you toast or fry it. It's culinary alchemy, as far as I'm concerned. Virtually inedible in its raw state, the salty Greek cheese transforms into something incredible when cooked and dressed with lime juice. The semi-sweet zing of the citrus cuts through the salt of the cheese to create a mouthwatering delight. A great little tapa!

Slice the cheese and brown it under the grill for a few minutes on each side. Serve warm, drizzled with the juice of the lime and sprinkled with fresh ground black pepper.

Tortilla

Tortilla, or Spanish omelette, is a really simple dish, delicious when eaten warm straight from the pan or cold on a picnic. Drizzled with a drop of honey, it can even make a fantastic breakfast. I like to use King Edward potatoes – or El Rey Eduardo, as the Spanish might call them – as they're my favourites, but any will do.

Peel and halve the potatoes. Heat the olive oil in a non-stick frying pan (you'll need a pan with fairly deep sides so that the omelette comes out like a cake). Slice the peeled potatoes thinly and simmer gently in the olive oil. Place a lid on the frying pan and continue to simmer for a good 5 minutes, or until the potato starts to soften.

Meanwhile, crack the eggs into a bowl and beat well. Add a pinch of salt and a good grind of black pepper. Pour the eggs over the potatoes. Lift the pan, and swirl the mixture around gently to make sure the egg covers all the potatoes. Turn the heat down and cook gently for 3 or 4 minutes, taking care not to let the tortilla burn.

To flip the tortilla, cover it with a plate and turn the pan over. Then slide the tortilla, uncooked side down, into the pan, and cook very gently for another 3 or 4 minutes.

Drink suggestion Simple whites and light reds go well with any kind of omelette – a Rueda Verdejo or another clean Spanish white would be ideal.

Ingredients Serves 2
- 2 or 3 large potatoes
- Olive oil
- 6 eggs
- Sea salt & fresh ground black pepper

Equipment
Sharp knife, high-sided, non-stick frying pan with lid, mixing bowl

Gambas al ajillo

Ingredients

Serves 4

- 2 tbsp olive oil
- 2 cloves garlic, finely chopped
- 500g fantail king/tiger prawns, cooked
- 1 level tsp hot smoked paprika
- Sea salt & fresh ground black pepper
- Fresh flat leaf parsley, chopped
- French bread (optional)

Equipment

Non-stick frying pan, sharp knife

My pal James suggested this recipe. It's his version of a dish he enjoyed in a London tapas bar. He stipulates using hot smoked paprika, which gives it a delicious smoky, spicy flavour – just right for the great outdoors. Using ready-cooked prawns makes it really easy and very quick indeed.

Serve the prawns with rounds of fresh crusty French bread for mopping up those juices.

Heat the olive oil in a non-stick frying pan until it's almost smoking, add the garlic and allow to sizzle until the aroma rises. Add the prawns and turn them in the hot oil, and then add the smoked paprika; heat the prawns in the spiced oil, turning them regularly. When they're heated through – say in around 2 to 3 minutes or so – check the seasoning (it will depend on how much salt the prawns were cooked in).

Garnish with a handful of chopped flat leaf parsley.

Drink suggestion Any crisp dry white will do nicely. Try a Muscadet or a Rueda Sauvignon.

Smoked salmon blinis

Blinis, beloved staple of fancy cocktail parties, are just tiny crumpets, as far as I can see. They're great to take camping, as they stay fresh for days and can be quickly warmed under a grill. You can top them with whatever you like, really, but I find a little roll of smoked salmon and cream cheese works well. Add a whole green olive for the continental effect!

Warm the blinis under the grill, top away – securing the olives with cocktail sticks – and tuck in.

Drink suggestion Babycham! Well, why not?

Ingredients Serves 4–6
- A packet of blinis
- Smoked salmon
- A tub of cream cheese (or a soft goat's cheese)
- Green olives

Equipment
Grill, cocktail sticks

41

Pancharagus

Ingredients

Serves as many as you like!

- Asparagus
- Pancetta
- Fresh ground black pepper
- Mayonnaise for dipping

Equipment

A griddle pan

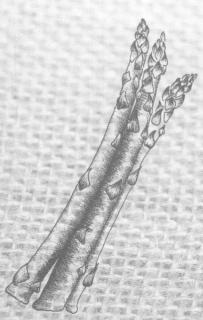

The idea for this came to me while I was doing a demonstration at Malton Food Festival one May – which, as it happens, coincides with the start of the British asparagus season. I needed a seasonal dish that was really quick, and with which I could both feed and entertain the Guyrope Gourmet audience. It's one of my many creations with a made-up name. (It was nearly called asparetta, but I think pancharagus sounds better.)

First "trim" the asparagus. Hold the tip in one hand, and the base of the stalk in the other. Carefully bend until the plant snaps. This is a great way of getting rid of the woody base of the asparagus – the snap will always occur at the top of the woody bit!

Carefully wrap a slice of pancetta around each spear of asparagus and cook for 2 or 3 minutes on a very hot griddle pan. You won't need any oil, as there is plenty in the pork. Roll the pancharagus over in the pan from time to time, so that the pancetta browns all round.

Season with black pepper and dip in a good mayonnaise.

Drink suggestion A good Sauvignon Blanc or Chablis.

44

Mushrooms with Parmesan and pancetta on toast

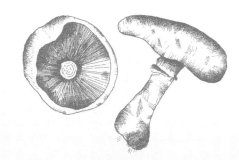

A great little lunch dish that takes just minutes to prepare – though you'll need a grill for the toast. The pancetta and light dusting of Parmesan really bring out the earthy flavour of the mushrooms. It doesn't matter what kind of mushrooms you use, but there is something extra special about using ones you've picked yourself – providing you know what you're picking, of course. I've used hand-picked giant puffball and broad field mushrooms, but this dish also works really well with king oyster mushrooms, which you might be lucky enough to find in a farmers' market.

It sits well on rye toast, but any good brown bread will work. I've tried it with white bread, but that tends to taste more transport café than camping treat!

Melt the butter in a non-stick frying pan, throw in the sprig of thyme and the sliced mushrooms and fry gently. While the mushrooms are cooking, grill the pancetta – it will only take a couple of minutes to get crispy, but don't burn it – and toast your bread at the same time.

Once the mushrooms have taken on some colour, remove the thyme. Pile the mushrooms on the toast and season to taste.

Place a couple of pieces of pancetta on top, dust with a little grated Parmesan, and garnish with the halved tomatoes.

Drink suggestion A light red – a young Pinot Noir, or a Valpolicella or Bardolino from Northern Italy – would be great, but a Macon Blanc or unoaked Chardonnay would go well too.

Ingredients Serves 2

- A large knob of butter (nothing else works quite as well)
- A small sprig of fresh thyme
- Fresh mushrooms of your choice, sliced
- Finely sliced pancetta (or thin-cut streaky bacon)
- Rye bread, or any other brown loaf
- Sea salt & fresh ground black pepper
- Parmesan cheese, grated
- Halved cherry or baby plum tomatoes

Equipment

Non-stick frying pan, grill, grater (if you need to grate the Parmesan)

Salads

ORGANIC FARM SHOP

UNDER A65 & TURN RIGHT

I'LL ALWAYS REMEMBER an episode at my small village primary school when I complained about having to eat a chicken salad on a cold winter's day. "This won't keep me warm," I moaned. Mrs Tidswell, the head dinner lady (and chef) soon put me straight with a withering look and a few words on the nutritional value of leaves. All that stuff about calories, energy expenditure and a balanced diet went over my head, I'm afraid – I was only eight years old, after all. Nowadays, though, I think of salad as an amazing dish, offering loads of reward in return for very little effort. It can be a quick standalone snack or it can accompany a bigger meal. All the dishes here – particularly the tabouleh, potato salad and coleslaw – keep really well in Tupperware containers in the camping coolbox.

Chorizo, potato and rocket salad

Ingredients Serves 4

- 8 or 9 baby new potatoes
- A chorizo ring (about 150g)
- 4 cloves of garlic
- Olive oil
- Sea salt & fresh ground black pepper
- 8 cherry tomatoes, halved
- A bag of rocket leaves

Equipment

Saucepan, sharp knife, strainer, non-stick frying pan, kitchen paper, serving bowl

A delicious, easy dish that works on its own and tastes great with chicken. The beauty of chorizo, a spicy cured Spanish sausage made with paprika, is that it will keep for a good few days in the coolbox. It's available in two forms – thinly sliced and packaged, or as a more traditional "ring" or long sausage. The latter works better for this salad, as its chunky texture goes particularly well with the potatoes.

Heat a saucepan of water and parboil the potatoes, whole, for 5 or 6 minutes. Don't overcook them – they should be firm when stabbed with a sharp knife and stick to the blade, rather than sliding off back into the pan.

While the spuds are cooking, cut the chorizo into small chunks and finely chop the garlic.

Once the potatoes are cooked, remove them from the heat, drain well and cut them into halves or quarters (you're looking for 2cm chunks).

Heat a glug of olive oil in a non-stick frying pan and add the potatoes and the chopped garlic, together with a pinch of salt and a grind of black pepper.

After a couple of minutes, add the chopped chorizo and cook gently for another 2 or 3 minutes until the paprika from the chorizo turns everything a delightful deep orange.

Spread out a couple of layers of kitchen paper in a bowl and tip in the chorizo and potatoes so that the paper absorbs some of the excess oil. Leave to cool for a minute while you are cutting the cherry tomatoes into halves.

Remove the kitchen paper from the bowl and add the halved tomatoes and the rocket leaves. Mix thoroughly, drizzle with a little olive oil and serve warm.

Drink suggestion A light red, a dry rosé or an unoaked white.

Broad bean and red onion salad with feta

Ingredients Serves 2

- A handful of fresh broad beans (probably about 300g in their pods). If you're using frozen beans you'll need a couple of handfuls (about 100g)
- 1 red onion
- A block of feta cheese, cubed
- A drizzle of olive oil
- Fresh ground black pepper

Equipment

Small saucepan, strainer, sharp knife

This was a "let's use up what we have left" recipe that made a lot of sense on a sunny day. Broad beans are one of my all-time favourite vegetables – I seem to have a few of those! – and while they're obviously at their best eaten on sunny days in season (June, July and August), like peas they freeze extremely well. The cooking method below assumes you're using fresh beans, but using frozen is just fine – not least because they'll help to keep your cooler chilled!

Shuck the beans (remove them from their pods) then blanch them in a small saucepan of boiling water for no more than 2 minutes. (Blanching is a way of cooking vegetables very quickly so that they maintain their colour – make sure the water is already boiling before you throw in the beans.)

Once blanched, drain the beans and allow them to cool a little. Remove the thick outer skin from each one to reveal a delicious-looking, bright green bean.

Peel, halve and finely slice the red onion, and toss it into a bowl along with the cubed feta. Drizzle with a little olive oil and season with black pepper (no need for salt – there's plenty in the feta).

Scatter the beans across the top of the salad and serve.

Drink suggestion A crisp dry white will suit this summery salad very well, matching the sharp and salty flavours – try an Alsace Riesling or a Sauvignon de Touraine.

Smoked chicken and avocado salad

Ingredients Serves 2

- A handful of rocket and salad leaves
- 1 smoked chicken breast, thinly sliced
- 1 avocado, peeled, stoned and thinly sliced
- ½ tsp honey mustard
- Olive oil
- Juice of half a lemon
- Sea salt & fresh ground black pepper

Equipment

Small plate, sharp knife

A great little salad, and one that can be prepared in a matter of minutes. I first put it together after a trip to a smokehouse while camping in North Yorkshire. Fascinated by the deep rusty hues of the oak-smoked chicken breast, I came away with a packet and got to thinking. The creamy flavour of the sliced avocado works well against the subtle, smoky chicken, and both are lifted by the bittersweet shenanigans of the honey mustard and lemon juice.

You can usually find smoked cooked chicken breast in farm shops, and some supermarkets stock it too. If a whole smoked breast is not available, go ahead and use the thin-sliced stuff.

Spread the salad leaves on a small plate and arrange the sliced chicken and avocado on top.

In a tumbler, mix the honey mustard with a good glug of olive oil and stir in the lemon juice. Season to taste, and drizzle over the salad.

Drink suggestion A light, dry and not too assertive, white — a Mâcon, perhaps, or an unoaked Chardonnay from the New World.

Potato salad

This is a delicious recipe that my step-mum Jude taught me. My cooking repertoire soared when Jude came along. Not only did she rescue my brother and I from my father's cooking and a diet of beefburgers and scrambled eggs, but she also taught me to think about pairing flavours. Here, the tartness of the chopped gherkins really lifts an otherwise simple salad.

This salad goes really well with a barbecue; the texture and flavour complement the smoky crispness of grilled meat brilliantly. It will also keep for a couple of days in a Tupperware container in the coolbox.

Boil the potatoes whole in a saucepan of lightly salted water for about 8 minutes. Cook until tender but not soft.

Drain and rinse the potatoes under cold water to stop the cooking process.

Allow the potatoes to cool and either halve or quarter them depending on their size.

Place the potatoes into a bowl and combine with the rest of the ingredients.

Drink suggestion A fine Spanish Albariño makes a great match for this simple salad.

Ingredients Serves 4
- A couple of handfuls of baby new potatoes
- 1 dessertspoon mayonnaise
- 1 dessertspoon plain yogurt
- A handful of cornichons or pickled gerkins, chopped
- A small bunch of spring onions, thinly sliced
- Fresh chives, chopped
- Sea salt & fresh ground black pepper

Equipment
Saucepan, sharp knife, mixing bowl

Tomato, mozzarella and basil

Ingredients
Serves 2 or 3

- 1 large beef tomato
- 1 packet of buffalo mozzarella
- A bunch of fresh basil
- Olive oil
- Sea salt & fresh ground black pepper

Drink suggestion

A Sauvignon Blanc will set off the tomatoes and the aromatic basil.

You'll laugh at this one. Call this a recipe? It's getting ridiculous. Joking aside, this is a fantastic and extremely quick side salad that works really well with barbecued meats. It looks pretty, too!

Cut the tomato into 2mm slices and lay them out on a plate.

Slice the mozzarella and place individual slices between the slices of tomato.

Rip whole basil leaves from the stem and place an individual leaf between the mozzarella and the tomato. This looks kind of nice, a little like the Italian flag (which is why they call it a tricolore salad in Italy!).

Drizzle a good glug of olive oil all around the plate and season to taste.

Coleslaw

Coleslaw is a true delight. I love grating carrots – there's something so satisfying about seeing the root disappear as you rub it against the grater (or is that just me?). Making your own coleslaw really doesn't take that much effort, and the results are always so much better than the shop-bought stuff. Be sure to allow enough time to let it stand for a while, though, as this gives the flavours a chance to fully develop.

This slaw will go with just about anything that you choose to cook on a barbecue.

Peel the two outer leaves from the cabbage and discard them. Cut the cabbage in half lengthwise and cut out the tough core at the base. Finely shred the leaves – it's worth taking some time with this, to get it as fine as you can. Place the shredded cabbage in a large bowl.

Finely chop the onion (again, as fine as you can), and add to the bowl, followed by the peeled and grated carrots.

Halve the apple and remove the core. Chop the halves into ½cm chunks, and add these to the bowl.

Add the mayonnaise and the yogurt, throw in the raisins and sunflower seeds and give it all a good stir, making sure that the mayo and yogurt are evenly distributed. Season with salt and black pepper to taste.

Let stand for at least 15 minutes before serving.

Drink suggestion Champagne goes rather well with coleslaw, but you could also enjoy a dry – but not bone-dry – fruity white.

Ingredients Serves 6

- 1 small white cabbage
- 1 medium onion (red ones look nice, but a white one will do)
- 2 large carrots, peeled and grated
- 1 apple (any of the "crunchy" varieties – Cox or Gala are ideal)
- 2 tbsp mayonnaise
- 1 tbsp plain yogurt
- A handful of raisins
- 1 small packet of sunflower seeds
- Sea salt & fresh ground black pepper

Equipment

Sharp knife, large bowl, grater

Feta, olive and red onion salad

Ingredients Serves 4

- 1 medium red onion
- A block of feta cheese (about 150g)
- A tin of pitted black olives
- A pinch of mixed dried herbs
- Olive oil
- Fresh ground black pepper

Equipment

A sharp knife

This tasty salad will happily sit alongside grilled fish or poultry or can even – with the addition of nothing more than a few crisp green lettuce leaves – make a meal in itself.

Peel, halve and finely slice the red onion. It's worth taking your time to cut really fine slices, as this will add to the flavour and the texture of the salad.

Cut the feta into 1cm cubes. Drain the tinned olives.

Combine all the ingredients in a salad bowl, and drizzle with good olive oil. Season with black pepper to taste and tuck in. No need to add any extra salt – the feta, which is cured in brine, is quite salty enough.

Drink suggestion The salty feta is the dominant flavour here, so you can't go wrong with a crisp dry white.

Tabouleh

A simple salad of bulgur wheat and chopped mint, with a few treats thrown in. The name comes from the Arabic verb "tabala", meaning to spice and season, and the fresh parsley and mint give the dish its zing. I consume tabouleh in quantity. It goes well with cooked meats (especially lamb) and works beautifully on its own. You can mess around with the quantities as you like, but here's the basic idea.

Place the bulgur wheat and a pinch of salt in a saucepan, and add water up to about 1cm above the wheat. Bring the water to the boil and reduce the heat to a very low simmer, until the water is absorbed – a matter of 5 minutes or so.

While the bulgur wheat is cooking, remove the stalks from the parsley and mint and chop the leaves finely. Slice the spring onions and chop the cucumber into small chunks. (I never peel cucumber, but you can do so if you wish.)

When cooked, the bulgur wheat should be white and firm but not crunchy to the bite. Drain it through a sieve and rinse with cold clean water. Drain very well again, and place in a bowl.

Quarter the tomatoes and add these, along with the chopped herbs, onions and cucumber, to the bowl with the bulgur wheat. Pour over a few good glugs of top-quality olive oil and squeeze in the juice of the lemon. Top with a grind of black pepper and mix well.

Let the tabouleh stand for at least 15 minutes to allow the flavours to develop before tucking in.

Drink suggestion Any light, dry white will work.

Ingredients Serves 4
- 250g bulgur wheat
- A bunch of fresh flat leaf parsley
- A bunch of fresh mint
- 6 spring onions
- ½ cucumber
- A few cherry tomatoes
- Lots of olive oil
- Juice of a lemon
- Sea salt & fresh ground black pepper

Equipment
Saucepan, sharp knife, sieve

Salsas Sauces & Dressings

SAUCES, DRESSINGS AND MARINADES
have the power to transform our food and add
mileage to a meal. A few crushed pine nuts
and fresh basil leaves will lift a plain bowl of
pasta to another level, while a dollop of zingy
tomato salsa on a homemade burger creates a
delicious barbecue classic. And what's a good
curry without a soothing raita to calm your
taste buds between mouthfuls of hot chillies?

Simple salad dressing

Ingredients

- 1 clove of garlic
- 5 tbsp olive oil
- 1 tbsp white wine vinegar
- 1 tsp wholegrain mustard
- Sea salt & fresh ground black pepper

A basic salad dressing can make a world of difference to a good salad. And good olive oil makes a world of difference to a basic salad dressing! Olive oil and balsamic vinegar alone will make the simplest of dressings, but I like to jazz things up a bit with garlic and mustard. The real key to making a good dressing is to get the oil to acid proportions right – as a rule, a 5:1 ratio will work.

Peel and crush the garlic clove and drop it into a small jug or a mug. Add the olive oil, vinegar and mustard, season to taste and stir well. Fish the crushed garlic out before pouring the dressing over your salad.

For a sweeter variation, you can add a teaspoon of honey mustard and use the juice of a lime instead of the vinegar.

Charmoula

Charmoula is a spicy, but not always hot, marinade used in North African cooking. It's a great word which, translated from the Arabic, has connotations of "uniting" and "gathering" – which is really appropriate for this delicious gathering of flavours. Charmoula works best with fish, but can be great with meat and vegetables too. Like any marinade, the longer you let the food steep in it, the better the end result.

Grind the cumin and coriander seeds together well in a pestle and mortar, throw in the clove of garlic and pinch of salt, and grind some more to achieve a dry paste.

Add the paprika, black pepper, olive oil and lemon juice. Mix well and finish with the fresh coriander.

Ingredients
This makes enough marinade to cover 2 large fillets of fish

- ¾ tsp whole cumin seeds
- 2 tsp whole coriander seeds
- 1 clove of garlic
- A pinch of sea salt
- 1 tsp paprika
- A grind of black pepper
- 4 tbsp olive oil
- Juice of a lemon
- A handful of fresh coriander, chopped

Equipment
Pestle and mortar, sharp knife

Raita

Ingredients Serves 4

- 350–400g plain yogurt
- ½ cucumber, diced
- A handful of cherry tomatoes, quartered
- 2 heaped tbsp grated fresh coconut (you can use creamed coconut instead, but as it has a more intense flavour you should reduce the amount slightly)
- 1 small onion, very finely chopped
- 5 or 6 spring onions, finely sliced
- Sea salt and fresh ground black pepper
- A pinch of paprika

Equipment

A sharp knife

My pal Glyn (pictured) grew up in India and watching him cook is a thing of wonder. This is his mother's recipe for raita, a yogurt dish that's terrific with most curries, makes a fine companion for grilled meats, works well with a spicy, cumin-infused couscous (see p111) and can even make a great salad dressing. The cherry tomatoes and grated coconut lift this version far beyond any I have sampled in an Indian restaurant.

Combine all the ingredients except the paprika in a bowl.

Dust with a pinch of paprika and allow to stand for at least 30 minutes — this gives the flavours a chance to develop.

Welsh red mustard mayonnaise

There's something very satisfying about making your own mayonnaise, especially on a campsite – it's easy to do, and just seems so gourmet! This recipe uses Welsh red mustard, which is a honey mustard that gets its vibrant colour from an extract of radish. It makes for a glorious orange mayo, but a teaspoon of English mustard powder will do fine if you're struggling to find the Welsh stuff. Homemade mayonnaise is best eaten on the day you make it.

Place the egg yolk in a bowl and beat with a little olive oil. Add the pinch of salt, the lemon juice and the mustard.

Place the bowl on a flat, stable surface (a grassy field is perfect, as it stops the bowl slipping all over the place). While beating with one hand, add the remaining olive oil in a fine drizzle. The mayonnaise will start to thicken.

Keep beating until you have added all of the oil and stop when you reach a consistency that you are happy with. Be careful not to overbeat, as the mayonnaise will split and end up lumpy. Add a grind of pepper before serving.

Ingredients Serves 4

- 1 egg yolk
- 100ml olive oil
- A pinch of salt
- 1 tsp lemon juice
- 1 tsp Welsh red mustard (or 1 tsp English mustard powder)
- A grind of black pepper

Equipment

An egg whisk

Tomato salsa

Ingredients Serves 4

- 6 tomatoes
- 6 spring onions
- 1 red onion
- ½ fresh red chilli
- 1 clove of garlic
- Sea salt & fresh ground black pepper
- 5 tbsp good olive oil
- Juice of 1 lime
- A good handful of fresh coriander, finely chopped

Equipment

A sharp knife

A bit on the faffy side, to use a technical term, but well worth the effort. Tomato salsa is brilliant with snacks, and if you're cooking tuna steaks (see p139) you'd be daft to ignore it. The longer the salsa gets to sit, the more delicious it is, and the key is to chop everything as finely as you can. That's why it's faffy, but all that chopping is essential for a good end result.

Quarter and de-seed the tomatoes. Chop them very finely and throw them into a bowl together with the finely sliced spring onions.

Peel and very finely chop the red onion. Very finely chop the de-seeded chilli and the garlic (notice the word *very*, in all cases).

Twist in a good grind of fresh milled black pepper and a pinch of flaked sea salt.

Add the olive oil and the lime juice.

Throw the finely chopped coriander into the bowl.

Stir well and leave to sit for at least 1 hour before serving.

Proper onion gravy

Gravy was one of the first things my mother showed me how to make, when I was about ten years old and, even today I find the whole process so satisfying that I rarely use granules. Onion gravy doesn't instantly spring to mind when most people think of camping food, granted, but this recipe is so simple that it deserves its place here. Besides, I don't see why we should be deprived of homely treats simply because we're sleeping in a field!

Heat the olive oil in the pan and fry the onion until it starts to take on colour. Add the knob of butter and the flour, stir well and cook for another 2 or 3 minutes.

Crumble in the stock cube and the dried herbs. Add the water a little at a time, stirring well to make sure that the mixture doesn't go lumpy.

Bring to the boil and turn down to a simmer. Cook until the gravy has thickened to your liking. Season to taste.

Ingredients Serves 4

- Olive oil
- 1 onion, finely sliced
- A knob of butter
- 1 tbsp plain flour
- 1 beef stock cube
- A pinch of dried mixed herbs
- 500ml vegetable water – if you're boiling potatoes or other vegetables as part of the meal, be sure to reserve the water and use it for the gravy
- Sea salt & fresh ground black pepper

Equipment

Sharp knife, high-sided, non-stick frying pan

Soups

SOUP IS THE FOOD OF CHAMPIONS –
and it's not just a winter thing. I honestly can't
remember there not being a pan bubbling
away on the stove while I was growing up.
And it's perfect for camping. It's easy to make,
usually cooked in just one pot – and, if you're
planning on getting active, you can pour it into
a Thermos flask to sustain you. (Soup tastes
even better on a bracing hike.) Once you get
the hang of a few basics, it's easy to create your
own recipe, and you can use practically any
ingredients you like.

Courgette and watercress soup

At home I usually use a blender for this one. However, given that not even I could bring myself to pack a food processor on a camping trip, a little improvisation goes a long way. By grating and then chopping the courgettes you'll end up with an acceptably chunky texture in a soup that is usually served liquidised.

This soup is particularly delicious when eaten with chunks of a crusty poppy-seed loaf.

In a large saucepan, heat a good glug of olive oil over a medium flame. Add the finely chopped onion and cook gently. After 4 or 5 minutes, as the onion begins to take on a little colour, add the grated and chopped courgette and give it all a good stir.

Add salt and pepper to taste – watercress has a peppery flavour, so bear that in mind as you are grinding those peppercorns.

Throw in the flour. This will help to thicken the soup. Cook the mixture gently, turning the flour through it until the courgette begins to wilt.

Add the stock, cover the saucepan with a lid and bring to the boil, then reduce the heat and simmer for 20 minutes.

Add the chopped watercress and simmer for a further 5 minutes.

Remove from the heat and stir in the double cream.

Ingredients Serves 6

- Olive oil
- 1 medium onion, finely chopped
- 6 courgettes, coarsely grated and chopped
- Sea salt & fresh ground black pepper
- 1 dessertspoon plain flour
- 1.5 ltr vegetable stock
- 2 bags of watercress, coarsely chopped
- 500ml double cream

Equipment

Sharp knife, large saucepan with lid, grater

Drink suggestion

A light, fruity, dry white or a light to medium red Chianti will go surprisingly well with this summery soup.

Tomato and roasted red pepper soup

Ingredients Serves 4

- 2 red peppers
- 2 tbsp olive oil
- 1 onion, finely chopped
- 1 clove of garlic, finely chopped
- 8 tomatoes, peeled and chopped
- 1 ltr boiling water
- 1 tbsp plain flour
- 2 tsp paprika
- 1 tsp bouillon powder
- Sea salt & fresh ground black pepper
- 1 tbsp chopped fresh chives (optional)
- A small pot of single cream (optional)

Equipment

Zip-lock plastic food bag, saucepan with lid, sharp knife, deep bowl

Tomato soup is wonderful stuff. When I was a kid, Dad invariably brought a flask of it along when we went for long walks. The flavour of a good tomato soup always reminds me of sitting by the waterfall at the top of the Valley of Desolation (which, in the Yorkshire Dales, is a lot more scenic than it sounds!). We'd warm our hands around the plastic cup and marvel at our surroundings. The chunky texture of this soup, together with the sweetness of the red peppers, makes for a real heartwarming treat.

Chargrill the peppers by placing them directly over the flame on the camping stove. Turn them regularly, until the skin becomes blackened and blistered on all sides (this will take 5 minutes or so). When done, seal the peppers in a zip-lock plastic food bag and allow them to cool (this makes it easier to remove the skins).

Heat the oil in a saucepan and add the onion. Cook gently until the onion begins to turn translucent and then add the chopped garlic. Cook some more until the onion turns a lovely golden colour.

While the onion and garlic are cooking, cut a small "X" on the bottom of each tomato and place them in a deep bowl. Cover the tomatoes with about a litre of boiling water.

Allow the tomatoes to stand for a few minutes until the skins begin to peel away. Remove the tomatoes from the water (keep the water) and allow them to cool.

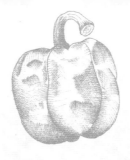

Peel and discard the tomato skins and then chop the tomatoes.

Add the flour, paprika, bouillon powder and a good pinch of salt to the onion and garlic and stir well. Cook for a couple of minutes more, stirring continually to prevent the mixture from sticking to the bottom of the pan.

Add the chopped tomatoes to the pan together with some of the reserved tomato water and stir.

Remove the peppers from the plastic bag and, using a knife, scrape off the charred black skin. It gets a bit messy, with the flakes of skin sticking to the knife, but don't worry about getting every last bit of black off. Just make sure you remove the majority of it.

Halve the peppers, and remove and discard the seeds. Finely chop the peppers and add them to the saucepan together with the rest of the tomato water. Place a lid on the pan and simmer very gently for 30 minutes. The soup will thicken and take on a beautiful deep red colour.

Season the soup to taste and garnish, if you wish, with a few chopped chives and a swirl of single cream.

Drink suggestion A dry white, maybe a Muscadet – or even a glass of Fino.

Stilton and leek soup

Ingredients Serves 4

- 50g butter or sunflower margarine (olive oil doesn't work with this, honest!)
- 500g leeks
- 500g floury potatoes
- 1 ltr vegetable stock
- 100g Stilton (discard the hard rind)
- 2 tbsp chopped fresh parsley
- Sea salt & fresh ground black pepper

Equipment

Sharp knife, saucepan

Drink suggestion

A Chardonnay or a robust Shiraz to balance the strong flavour of the Stilton.

Thanks to my friend James for this delightfully simple interpretation of a classic. I'll let you into a secret; this is what I am stirring on the cover of this book! I loved the rather mechanical and direct tone in James's cooking instructions, so while I've tweaked the ingredients list, I've kept the method more or less as James wrote it down. Serve with the freshest bread you can get your hands on.

Melt butter or margarine, shred leeks finely – cook until softened.

Add potatoes, diced small, and cook for 5 minutes.

Add hot stock and bring to the boil. Simmer for 30 minutes or so until the vegetables are very soft. Mash the potatoes into the soup to thicken the texture.

Crumble in the Stilton little by little, tasting as you go. Stilton can vary greatly in strength so when you have reached a balance you are happy with, stop.

You can add cream, but I don't think it needs it. Add the chopped parsley, season to taste.

Pea and ham soup

Ingredients Serves 4

- 1 tbsp olive oil
- 1 large onion, finely chopped
- 225g split red lentils
- Fresh ground black pepper
- A handful of fresh flat leaf parsley, chopped

For the stock:

- 1 ham hock (around 1 or 1.5kg in weight)
- 2 sticks of celery, roughly chopped
- 1 carrot, peeled and sliced
- 1 small onion, halved, skin left on
- 6 whole black peppercorns
- 2 star anise
- water

Equipment

Sharp knife, stockpot with lid, large saucepan with lid, slotted spoon, sieve or colander

This is my take on my mother-in-law's recipe. Eileen was a latecomer to the camping lark; she coined the term "gramping" a couple of years ago, and joined us on a few trips. She even reached the giddy heights of fame, appearing in a feature in *Camping Magazine*, no less. My kids loved having Grandma around the camp, and I'll never forget the relief on her face when she realised that there were actually hot showers and loos on the site.

I rarely add salt to this recipe, as the ham hock can be very salty to start with. It's wonderful served with crusty bread.

First make the stock. Place the ham hock, celery, carrot and onion in a stockpot with the peppercorns and star anise.

Add enough water to cover the hock (about 1.5ltr, depending on the size of your pot), cover with a lid and bring to the boil. Reduce the heat to a low simmer and leave the stock to cook for 45 minutes.

Meanwhile, in a separate large saucepan, heat the olive oil and gently fry the chopped onion until it begins to take on colour. Add the lentils and stir well. Turn off the heat.

Once the stock is ready, remove the lid from the stockpot and lift out the ham hock with a slotted spoon. Set it aside to cool and strain the remaining stock into the saucepan that contains the lentils and onion.

Bring to the boil (this won't take very long at all, as the stock will still be hot), reduce the heat to a gentle simmer and cover the saucepan with a lid.

Once the ham hock is cool enough to handle, cut away the skin and discard it. Next, strip the meat from the bone and chop it roughly.

Add the chopped ham to the saucepan with the lentils and stock and continue to cook until the lentils lose their shape and go very soft. Let the soup thicken for around 30 minutes. Stir from time to time, adding more water if necessary.

Season the soup with black pepper and serve garnished with flat leaf parsley.

Drink suggestion A fruity red, perhaps a Merlot, would work well.

Oxtail soup

Ingredients Serves 4

- 1 tbsp olive oil
- 1kg oxtail, cut into chunks
- 1 large onion, finely chopped
- 2 cloves of garlic, finely chopped
- 4 celery stalks, chopped
- 1 large carrot, peeled and sliced
- Sea salt & fresh ground black pepper
- 1 heaped tsp paprika
- 1 tbsp plain flour
- 1 beef stock cube
- A large glass of red wine
- 2 star anise
- 1 bay leaf

Equipment

Large stockpot with lid, large bowl, sharp knife

Drink suggestion

Match this rich soup with an Australian Shiraz or a warming southern French red – perhaps a Corbières or Minervois.

Oxtail soup takes me back to the late 1970s. Every Wednesday evening after swimming lessons, we were allowed to have a cup of it from the vending machine at the baths. I remember holding the hot cup in both hands and blowing at it gently, sipping slowly in a desperate bid to warm up.

In an attempt to recreate the warming joy that oxtail soup can bring, I thought I'd have a go at making it on a campsite, where you often have to keep shivers at bay, even in the height of summer. This dish does take a while to cook, and the longer you cook it the better it tastes. If you're lucky enough to be on a campsite that allows campfires it's perfect, as you can leave it to simmer for ages without worrying about using up all of your gas. As far as I can see, this is what a Kotlich and tripod were made for. . .

If fires are forbidden on your campsite, then a good hour on a camp stove will see a tasty soup to stave off the cold.

Heat the olive oil in a large stockpot. Brown the chunks of oxtail on all sides, remove and set aside in a large bowl.

Add the finely chopped onion and garlic to the pot, and cook them in the remaining olive oil. Add the chopped celery and sliced carrot. Throw in a good pinch of sea salt and a generous grind of black pepper. Add the paprika and stir well. Place a lid on the stockpot and let the vegetables soften a little.

Add the flour and the crumbled beef stock cube to the pot. Stir the whole thing well, making sure the flour is evenly distributed. Pour in a little of the red wine and stir again. The ingredients will feel quite thick and sticky, but will loosen up as you slowly pour in the rest of the wine, which you should do at this stage.

Return the oxtail to the stockpot, making sure that you pour in any of the juices that have gathered at the bottom of the bowl. Add the star anise and the bay leaf. Pour in enough water to just cover the chunks of oxtail (about 1 litre), give it one last stir and simmer very gently over a low heat for at least an hour – or as long as you possibly can!

After a couple of hours the meat will fall off the bones and the whole thing becomes deliciously unctuous. Once the meat has fallen away, take out the bones, scrape off any last strands of meat and add them to the pot. Remove the star anise and the bay leaf (if you can find them!) and serve.

Stews & Casseroles

THE STEW GOT SHORT SHRIFT in my kitchen for far too many years. I think it's to do with the word itself, conjuring up images of grey prison food and orphaned Dickensian scoundrels. Thankfully my travels in the Middle East put paid to those associations and opened my eyes to this fantastic way of preparing good, simple food. A pot of stew or a hearty casserole can keep, with the lid on, for a couple of days, and will taste great when heated up the second time round. The following dishes are really easy and make for a terrific-looking meal, especially when cooked with good fresh ingredients grown within miles of your campsite.

Simple lamb stew

Ingredients Serves 4

- Olive oil
- 2 medium onions, chopped
- 3 cloves of garlic, finely chopped
- 500g diced lamb (leg is good)
- Sea salt & fresh ground black pepper
- ½ glass of red wine
- ½ beef stock cube
- 1 tsp paprika
- 3 carrots, peeled and sliced
- 12 baby new potatoes, whole
- A sprig of fresh thyme
- A sprig of fresh rosemary

Equipment

Sharp knife, saucepan with lid

This is a hearty dish and, as the name suggests, one that's really simple to prepare. It's a regular for me – I often cook it at home the day before a camping trip and reheat it once we get to the campsite, particularly if we're arriving late on a Friday night and need to eat quickly and get the kids tucked up in their sleeping bags.

Serve with crusty bread (and tired children!).

Heat the olive oil in a saucepan and cook the chopped onions over a medium flame for a good 5 minutes.

While the onions are simmering, finely chop the garlic and add it to the pan along with the diced lamb. Add a good grind of black pepper and a pinch of salt and stir, making sure that the meat is sealed on all sides.

Pour in the wine, crumble in the beef stock cube and add the paprika. Peel the carrots and slice (about 2cm slices), and then add to the pan with the whole potatoes. Throw in the fresh thyme and rosemary and add a little more than 500ml water. Bring to the boil and then reduce the heat to a gentle simmer for 30 minutes.

Drink suggestion A Côtes du Rhône, Cabardès or other southern French red.

Flexible fish stew

Another deliciously simple stew, which works particularly well if you go to the trouble of making the stock first. You could use stock powder or cubes, but I guarantee it won't taste as good. Don't worry about getting the seafood ingredients spot on, though. You really can use whatever you happen to get hold of. Mussels would work, and you could throw in a handful of cockles or other clams if you feel so inclined. King prawns are good too. If monkfish is too expensive, use something else. It really is, after all, a flexible fish stew.

Ingredients Serves 2

For the stock
- 2 or 3 langoustines
- 1 bunch of spring onions, chopped
- ½ bulb of fennel, chopped
- Sea salt
- 6 whole black peppercorns
- Fresh tarragon
- 4 or 5 dried mushrooms (or half a dozen fresh ones), coarsely chopped
- 500ml water

For the fish stew
- ½ bulb of fennel, chopped
- Olive oil
- A knob of butter
- 1 tsp paprika
- Fresh ground black pepper
- 1 tin of tomatoes
- 6 baby new potatoes (Jersey Royals, if available), halved
- 1 small fillet of haddock
- 1 small fillet of monkfish
- 3 or 4 king scallops
- 12 queen scallops
- Fresh tarragon
- 4 cherry tomatoes, halved

Equipment
Two large saucepans with lids, sharp knife, sieve, wooden spoon

For the stock

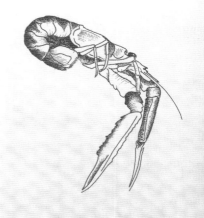

If you choose to use stock cubes or powder to make your stock, make up 500ml, set it aside, and go straight to the instructions overleaf.

To make a fresh stock, cook the langoustines, if using, by boiling them in a saucepan of salted water for 5 minutes or so. Remove the claws and heads for use in the stock, and set the tails aside for use in the stew.

Chop the green ends of the spring onions (set aside the white ends for the stew) and place in a separate saucepan along with the coarsely chopped fennel, a pinch of sea salt and the whole black peppercorns. Throw in the langoustine claws and heads together with a sprig of tarragon and the mushrooms.

Add 500ml of water and bring to the boil. Reduce the heat to a gentle simmer and cook the stock with a lid on for 20 to 30 minutes. Strain the stock through a sieve and set aside for adding to the stew.

Continues overleaf

To make the base for the stew

Finely chop the fennel together with the reserved white ends of the spring onions. Heat a glug of olive oil and a knob of butter in a saucepan and throw in the fennel and spring onions. Simmer for 5 minutes then add the teaspoon of paprika and a good twist of ground black pepper.

Pour in the tinned tomatoes and add about half of the prepared stock. Break up the tomatoes with a wooden spoon while stirring. Simmer with the lid on for 5 minutes, stirring occasionally.

Add the halved baby new potatoes and the rest of the stock, replace the lid and continue to simmer for another 5 minutes or until the potatoes are nearly cooked through.

Cut the fish into large chunks and add to the pan together with the king scallops.

After a couple of minutes add the queen scallops – these are much smaller and will need less time to cook. Throw in two or three sprigs of tarragon and simmer for a couple more minutes.

Finally, add the cooked langoustine tails to warm through.

Garnish the stew with the halved cherry tomatoes and a scattering of tarragon.

Drink suggestion A smart dish deserves a smart wine, but the flavour of tarragon can clash. A softer Sauvignon – from Chile or South Africa rather than France or New Zealand – should work, or you could try a Rueda.

Chicken and chorizo casserole

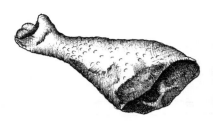

This is a fantastic feast that my pal Niki Jones rustled up for us all on a windswept and rainy campsite in mid Wales. "You sort the kids, I'll sort the supper," she said as the wind lashed around the flysheet and my children burst into tears. Niki is a teacher – she's used to sorting things out – and her words were music to my ears on that particular occasion! I'm a big fan of chorizo. It gives this casserole a subtle, smoky flavour that warms you up and drives off inclement weather.

Heat a couple of tablespoons of olive oil in a stockpot over a good flame, and add the chopped onion and garlic. Cook gently for 4 or 5 minutes.

Add the chopped peppers and the chicken joints. Turn the chicken so it begins to brown all over. As the onion becomes translucent, throw in the flour and paprika. The whole thing will turn a glorious orange colour.

Now add the chopped chorizo and marvel as the colour deepens. Chuck in the red wine and the chopped tomatoes. Give it all a good stir and bring back to a simmer.

Stir in the vegetable stock and add salt and pepper to taste and a glass of water for good measure.

Place a lid on the pot and turn the flame to low. Simmer for 45 minutes, stirring occasionally so as not to let it stick and burn on the bottom of the pot.

Drink suggestion If you can find one, a red Irouléguy from the Basque border between France and Spain would be perfect. Otherwise a fruity red from Navarra, a young Rioja or a wine from La Mancha would do the trick.

Ingredients Serves 6

- Olive oil
- 1 large onion, finely chopped
- 2 cloves of garlic, finely chopped
- 1 red pepper, chopped
- 1 yellow pepper, chopped
- 6 joints of fresh chicken (drumsticks, thighs or both)
- 1 heaped tsp plain flour
- 1 dessertspoon paprika
- Half a chorizo ring, chopped
- 1 small glass of red wine
- 1 tin of chopped tomatoes
- 1 ltr vegetable stock (use a stock cube or a heaped tsp of bouillon)
- Sea salt & fresh ground black pepper

Equipment

Sharp knife, large stockpot with lid

Simple beef and ale stew

Ingredients Serves 4

- Olive oil
- 1 large onion, roughly chopped
- 1 clove of garlic, chopped
- 500g stewing steak, cubed
- Sea salt & fresh ground black pepper
- 2 tsp plain flour
- A 500ml bottle of ale of your choice (I like a honeyed ale, such as Fullers Honeydew. If you use Guinness, throw in ¼ tsp of sugar to counter the bitterness of the stout)
- 500ml water
- A handful of small new potatoes
- A sprig of fresh thyme
- 1 bay leaf

Equipment

Heavy, deep saucepan – ideally cast iron – with a tight-fitting lid, sharp knife

This is a really easy camping dish that always comes up trumps in terms of flavour. The secret is to cook it slowly; an hour will do the trick. One tip, though it pushes the price up, is to use a tender lean cut of steak, such as topside – this allows you to cut down a little on the cooking time and save gas.

Enjoy with hunks of crusty bread and steamed greens.

Heat the olive oil and cook the chopped onion over a medium heat for 5 minutes. Add the chopped garlic and stir. Cook until the onion begins to take on a little colour.

Throw in the cubed stewing steak and stir, making sure the meat seals on all sides. Add a pinch of salt and a good grind of black pepper. Sprinkle in the flour and stir, ensuring it coats the meat well. Cook for a further 3 or 4 minutes, stirring occasionally. The flour will start to stick to the bottom of the pan but don't worry – it will loosen up once you add the ale and the water.

Pour in the ale and about 500ml water, and add the new potatoes, thyme (stalk and all) and bay leaf. Give the whole thing a good stir, making sure you scrape the bottom of the pan well. Place the lid on the pan and turn to a very gentle simmer. Cook for 1hr.

The stew will thicken nicely as it cooks. If it too thick, add a little more water; if it's too thin, simmer gently with the lid off for a while. Don't forget to fish out the thyme stalk and the bay leaf before serving.

Drink suggestion Beer, naturally – preferably a hearty local ale. Non beer-drinkers should go for a light red wine – anything with too much tannin will clash. Try a Zinfandel from California.

Rapid ratatouille

I'm afraid I'm of an age when I can't think about ratatouille without thinking about *Fawlty Towers*. Each time I make it, I say out loud in my best (worst) Spanish accent, "you put basil in the ratatouille?" (Which you don't.) It's all a bit complicated if you haven't seen it, but the joke revolves around hapless Spanish waiters, bullying hoteliers, and an escaped pet rat.

Seventies sit-coms aside, this is a colourful, hearty dish that's particularly well suited to the camp stove, as you don't need to cook it for hours. (Some purists might argue otherwise, but I like the veg in my ratatouille to keep their colour.)

Sauté the chopped onion and garlic in a little olive oil until they begin to caramelise. Add the sliced courgettes, the sliced, quartered aubergine and the sliced red peppers. Throw in the fresh herbs (leave the stalks on – you can pick them out at the end) and the paprika.

Quarter the tomatoes and grate them into the pan. This is a good way of getting rid of the tomato skins without having to steep them in boiling water and peel them. If you opt for tinned tomatoes, simply sling the contents into the pan.

Season the mixture with salt and pepper, stir and simmer gently until the vegetables are cooked. I like my pepper to have a little bite, so 20 minutes or so is fine in my book – you may wish to simmer your ratatouille for a little longer.

Drink suggestion Southern French reds or red Rhônes with plenty of fruit go beautifully with this classic dish.

Ingredients Serves 4

- Olive oil
- 1 large onion, chopped
- 2 cloves of garlic, finely chopped
- 2 courgettes, sliced
- 1 large aubergine, sliced and quartered
- 2 red peppers, de-seeded and sliced lengthwise
- A sprig of fresh rosemary
- A sprig of fresh thyme
- A pinch of paprika
- 6 tomatoes (you could use a tin if you like)
- Sea salt & fresh ground black pepper

Equipment

Sharp knife, heavy-based frying pan, grater (if using fresh tomatoes)

Middle Eastern lamb stew with shredded ginger and fennel

Syria is an amazing country, not least for its cuisine. I lived in Damascus for a year, and lamb stew – invariably accented with the flavours of cumin and fresh coriander – was a staple. I must have eaten my way through a whole flock while I was there. After years trying to replicate my Damascene dining experience, I found that messing about with and adding grated fennel to Jamie Oliver's recipe from his first book *The Naked Chef* got me the closest. This stew goes brilliantly with couscous (see p110).

Ingredients Serves 4

- 1 tsp cumin seeds
- 1 tbsp fennel seeds
- 2 tbsp coriander seeds
- 500g fresh lamb neck fillets
- 1 tbsp olive oil
- 1 large onion, finely chopped
- 4 cloves of garlic, chopped
- ½ dried red chilli, finely chopped
- 1 large aubergine, chopped
- 1 tin of plum tomatoes
- Sea salt & fresh ground black pepper
- 1 tin of chickpeas
- 100g fresh root ginger (a piece about the size of a small child's hand), peeled and grated
- ½ bulb of fennel, grated
- A bunch of fresh coriander, chopped

Equipment

Pestle and mortar, sharp knife, large bowl, large stockpot with lid

Crush the cumin and fennel seeds in a pestle and mortar, and then add the coriander seeds. Grind the lot so that there are no whole seeds remaining (you're after sawdust rather than a fine powder).

Cut the lamb neck fillets into 2cm chunks and place them in a bowl with the crushed seeds. Give it a good mix around with your hand, making sure every piece of meat is coated with the spice mixture.

Heat the olive oil in a large stockpot, add the chopped onion and cook over a low heat until it begins to take on a little colour. Add the chopped garlic, turn up the heat a little and add the chopped chilli and the meat. Brown the meat on all sides.

Chop the aubergine into 2cm chunks, add it to the meat mixture and stir. Turn the heat down and add the tin of tomatoes with a little water. Season to taste and cover the stockpot with a lid. Simmer gently for 30 minutes, stirring occasionally.

Add the drained tin of chickpeas together with the peeled and coarsely grated ginger and the coarsely grated fennel. Cook for a further 10 minutes, add the chopped fresh coriander, stir and remove from the heat. Let stand for 2 or 3 minutes before serving.

Drink suggestion The ginger would be set off nicely by a soft red from Italy or something red and fruity from the South of France.

Rice & Couscous

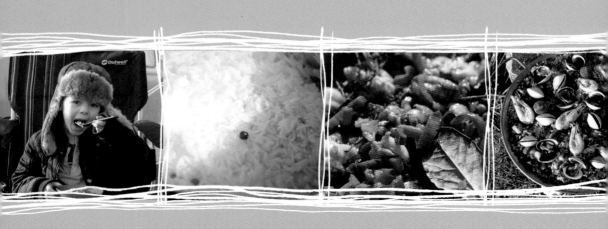

WITH A BAG OF RICE or a jar of couscous in the camping larder you simply can't go wrong. They're superb staples, and sit well with a wide range of dishes from fish or meat to chargrilled vegetables. A risotto or a pilaf can be ready in less than half an hour, while couscous will cook in a fraction of that time, absorbing the flavours of whatever you serve it with. Perfect for quick, filling meals.

Perfect rice

Ingredients Serves 4

- 450ml water
- 225g basmati rice
- 1 star anise
- 6 whole black peppercorns
- 1 bay leaf
- 1 tsp boullion powder or vegetable stock powder
- Pinch of flaked sea salt
- Drizzle of olive oil

Equipment

Measuring jug, saucepan with lid, clean tea towel

A subtly flavoured rice that's good with curries, cutlets, spicy prawns – in fact, it's good with just about anything. This is a really simple method, and it works time after time – you will need a measuring jug, though, as the secret (or at least part of the magic) is the precise twice-the-liquid-to-rice ratio. Oh, and you should always make sure you use basmati rice; other types just don't get the same results.

Measure out the water in a jug and put it, with all the other ingredients (except the olive oil) into a saucepan. Cover with a lid and bring to the boil. Turn to a low heat and leave to simmer very gently for 15 minutes.

Remove the lid and stir gently with a fork. You will see that the majority of the liquid has been absorbed.

Fold the tea towel in half and place it over the pan. Put the lid back on and press it into place to give a tight fit. Fold the hanging corners of the tea towel up onto the pan lid to stop them going up in flames. Continue to simmer the rice over a very low heat for a further 5 minutes.

Turn off the heat and leave the pan to stand, unopened, for another 5 minutes or until you are ready to serve.

Remove the lid and tea towel, add the drizzle of olive oil and fork through. The rice will be unbelievably light and fluffy. Fish out the bay leaf and star anise – and smile.

Chickpea and apricot pilaf

I bagged this from campervan owner and fine food connoisseur Alan Harrison. I'd spotted his tweet about a dish he'd made on a road trip in his campervan, Chalky. I loved the sound of cinnamon with apricots and almonds and immediately asked him for the recipe. It's great with lamb chops, when it gets a kind of Middle Eastern thing going.

Heat the olive oil in a large saucepan and cook the sliced onion and chopped garlic until soft. Add the cinnamon and tomato purée and stir in the basmati rice. Add the stock to cover the rice and simmer gently for 10 to 15 minutes.

Add the chickpeas along with the chopped apricots and almonds. Simmer for a further 5 minutes and add the fresh coriander to serve.

Drink suggestion Pilaf, like couscous, likes a good warm red. Don't choose anything too dry for this dish, though, as it could clash with the sweetness of the apricot.

Ingredients Serves 4

- Olive oil
- 1 large onion, thinly sliced
- 2 cloves of garlic, finely chopped
- 2 tsp ground cinnamon
- 2 tbsp tomato purée
- 250g basmati rice
- 500ml vegetable stock
- 1 tin of chickpeas, drained
- A handful of chopped, dried apricots
- A handful of chopped almonds
- Fresh coriander, chopped

Equipment
Sharp knife, large saucepan

Pea and broad bean risotto

Ingredients Serves 2
- 1.5 ltr water
- 1kg fresh garden peas (in pods)
- 1kg fresh broad beans (in pods)
- Vegetable stock cube or bouillon powder
- Olive oil
- 1 onion, finely chopped
- 200g Arborio risotto rice
- Sea salt & fresh ground black pepper
- 1 large glass of dry white wine
- 2 tbsp grated Parmesan cheese
- A large knob of butter

Equipment
Saucepan, sieve, sharp knife, jug for the vegetable water

The simplest risottos are usually the best. With new-season legumes arriving from April/May onwards, this recipe is a must for early summer evenings and follows the principles of any basic risotto – don't over-complicate. You need a good glass of white wine (both for cooking and for drinking).

Bring the water to the boil in a pan. While the water is heating, shell the peas and beans. Once the water comes to the boil, toss them into the pan and simmer for 3 minutes. You want the vegetables to be al dente, so don't overdo it.

Drain the peas and beans but keep the water for stock. That bit is important, so I'll say it again: keep the water for stock! Pick out the broad beans and remove the husks. It's easy, if a bit fiddly: just pinch a slit with your thumbnail and squeeze the bright green bean from the outer skin. It'll be well worth the effort – those tough skins taste bitter. Set the vegetables aside and add a couple of teaspoons of bouillon or a stock cube to the vegetable water.

Heat the oil in the saucepan and cook the chopped onion until it begins to soften and turn a lovely golden colour.

Throw in the rice and stir. Add a pinch of salt and fresh ground black pepper. Add the glass of wine, and stir again.

Pour in the stock a little at a time and stir well, simmering until all the liquid is absorbed and the rice begins to soften. The more you stir the better this gets!

Once the rice loses its nutty crunch, add the peas and beans and grated Parmesan. Stir well, remove the pan from the heat and allow to stand for 2 or 3 minutes.

Stir in the knob of butter before serving.

Drink Suggestion A crisp, dry white – Albariño for me every time. Otherwise, perhaps a Verdicchio or a Fiano di Avellino from Italy.

Ingredients Serves 4

- 100g green beans, trimmed and halved
- 1 small aubergine, diced
- 1 carrot, peeled and sliced
- 1 small cauliflower, cut into small florets
- 1 sweet potato, peeled and cut into 2cm chunks
- 200g waxy potatoes, peeled and diced
- 200g butter
- 1 large onion, peeled and chopped
- 4 cardamom pods
- 1 tsp cumin seeds
- 6 whole black peppercorns
- 2cm piece of fresh ginger, peeled and finely chopped
- ¼ tsp turmeric
- ½ tsp chilli powder
- 1 tsp garam masala
- 4 tbsp natural yogurt
- Sea salt
- 500g basmati rice
- 4 tbsp fresh coriander, chopped
- 1 cinnamon stick
- A pinch of saffron threads
- 150ml milk
- 2 green chillies, de-seeded and finely chopped
- Juice of ½ lemon

Vegetable biryani

The first time I made this biryani, at a cooking demonstration a couple of years ago, I carefully followed Shehzad Husain's recipe from her fine tome *An Indian Table*. It worked really well, and I made so much of it that everyone got to try some.

Since then I've messed around with it a bit, adding a few of my own preferred vegetables and altering the quantities a little. There's a lot of preparation to do up front, but that can make it a great camping dish; it's fun to sit around camp preparing vegetables, drinking a glass of wine and chatting with your fellow campers. Once the prep is done, it's reasonably straightforward. Oh, and yes, it really does need that much butter!

If you really want to impress, you could make a raita (see p62) to go with your biryani. It's a brilliant combination.

Place all the prepared vegetables, except for the onion, into a mixing bowl.

Melt the butter in a large saucepan and add the onion, two of the cardamom pods, the cumin seeds and the peppercorns. Simmer until the onion turns golden brown. Add the vegetables to the pan and stir through the butter.

Mix the ginger, turmeric, chilli powder and garam masala with the yogurt and add to the pan.

Throw in a good pinch of salt, cook for a couple of minutes and remove from the heat.

Place the rice in the stockpot and pour in water until there is about 3cm of water above the rice.

Put half the fresh coriander, the remaining two cardamom pods and the cinnamon stick in with the rice and bring to the boil. Turn the heat down and simmer for 10 minutes. You want the rice to be half cooked, so it should still be crunchy to the bite.

While the rice is cooking, grind up the saffron in the pestle and mortar and add it to the milk in a cup. Add a couple of tablespoons of hot rice water to the cup and let the saffron infuse.

When the rice has been simmering for 10 minutes, remove half of it from the stockpot and set aside. Place all of the vegetables on top of the rice that is remaining in the pot, but save some of the buttery onion. Add a handful of the remaining coriander. Pour in half of the saffron-infused milk and add one of the chopped green chillies, then squeeze in the lemon juice.

Plonk the remaining rice back in the pot to cover the vegetables. Pour over the rest of the saffron milk and add the last of the buttery onion. Scatter with the remaining handful of coriander and cover with a tight-fitting lid.

Place the pot back over a low heat and cook without stirring for another 20 minutes. Remove from the heat and allow to stand for 5 minutes before serving onto warm plates.

Drink suggestion A nice cold Cobra lager.

Equipment
Sharp knife, mixing bowl, large saucepan, large stockpot with lid, pestle and mortar

A paella of sorts

This is one of my favourite things to cook. I love the fact that you build a paella – it becomes more and more substantial as you add the ingredients – and that it turns out slightly different every time. Good paella is often about the pan you cook it in. A proper paella pan has lots of tiny indentations all over the bottom, which help the rice to cook evenly. If you don't have one, then a large, high-sided frying pan will do.

It really is worth spending the extra cash (about a quid) on Bomba paella rice. Grown around the Valencia region of Spain, which is the home of paella, it holds its shape well when cooked and has a reassuring firmness to the bite. If you can't find it, then you can get away with Arborio risotto rice.

Ingredients Serves 4

- Olive oil
- 1 large red onion, finely chopped
- 1 red pepper (or green, or yellow – *es egual!*), halved, de-seeded and sliced
- 2 cloves of garlic, finely chopped
- ¼ dried chilli, de-seeded and finely chopped
- 3 or 4 large flat mushrooms
- 100g chorizo
- 2 chicken breasts
- A large knob of butter
- 1 tsp paprika
- Sea salt & fresh ground black pepper
- 225g Bomba paella rice
- A glass of Manzanilla sherry or very dry white wine
- 500ml vegetable stock
- 6 or 8 cooked whole shell-on prawns
- Fresh flat leaf parsley, chopped
- A few tomatoes, quartered
- 1 lemon, cut into wedges

Equipment
Kettle, sharp knife, paella pan or large high-sided frying pan

Boil a kettle for the vegetable stock.

Heat a glug of olive oil in a paella pan, add the finely chopped onion and cook gently for 4 or 5 minutes. When the onion begins to soften, throw in the sliced pepper, the garlic and the chilli. Cook for a further 3 or 4 minutes, taking care not to burn the garlic.

Meanwhile, slice the mushrooms and chop the chorizo and chicken into 1cm chunks. Add the knob of butter to the pan and throw in the mushrooms. Then add the chorizo and chicken, turning to make sure the chicken seals on all sides.

Add the paprika, a pinch of sea salt and a good grind of fresh black pepper.

Add the rice to the pan and stir well, ensuring it is well coated. Add the sherry or wine and stir. Pour in the vegetable stock and bring to the boil. Reduce to a gentle simmer for 20 minutes or so, or until the rice has absorbed all of the stock and is soft to the bite. You may need to add a little water from time to time if the rice is too al dente.

Place the cooked prawns on top of the paella to warm through for 3 or 4 minutes before the rice is fully cooked.

Finally, drizzle with olive oil and garnish with the chopped parsley, tomatoes and lemon wedges.

Drink suggestion A good Spanish wine, be it a Cava, a Rueda, an Albariño or a dry rosé. If you prefer red, it should be on the lighter side – but I'd stick to white.

Mushroom and fennel risotto with asparagus

Ingredients Serves 4

- 3 tbsp olive oil
- A large knob of butter
- 1 onion, finely chopped
- 1 small bulb of fennel, finely chopped
- 3 cloves of garlic, finely chopped
- Sea salt & fresh ground black pepper
- 4 large flat field mushrooms, chopped
- 100g mixed fresh wild mushrooms, chopped (add a couple more field mushrooms if you can't lay your hands on wild varieties)
- 225g Arborio risotto rice
- ½ glass of white wine
- 1 sprig of fresh thyme
- 1 ltr vegetable stock
- 50g Parmesan cheese, grated, plus extra to serve
- 1 bunch of asparagus tips

Equipment

High-sided frying pan with a lid, sharp knife

Risotto purists might bemoan the fact that I'm not imploring you to stir this dish until your arms grow tired. But this is the simplified version – the only stirring that needs to be done is after you've added the Parmesan, when you need to make sure the rice doesn't stick to the bottom of the pan during the final stage of cooking.

The earthy flavour of the mushrooms works really well with the sharpness of the fennel. Adding steamed asparagus on top just adds pleasure to perfection!

Heat the olive oil and melt the butter in a high-sided frying pan. Add the chopped onion and cook gently with a lid on for 5 minutes.

Add the chopped fennel and garlic and cook for a further 10 minutes. Season with sea salt and fresh black pepper.

Chop the flat mushrooms into 1cm chunks and roughly chop the wild mushrooms. Add to the frying pan and simmer with the lid on. The mushrooms will start to soften and the contents of the pan will turn a rich, dark brown.

Throw in the rice and the white wine, add the sprig of fresh thyme and stir thoroughly, making sure the rice is well coated with the other contents of the pan.

Add the stock and bring to the boil. Reduce the heat and simmer very gently with the lid on for 10 minutes.

Stir in the grated Parmesan cheese and throw the asparagus tips on top of the rice. Replace the lid and simmer gently for a further 10 minutes, or until the rice is soft to bite. Stir every now and again, to make sure the rice does not stick to the bottom of the pan. You may need to add a little more water if it appears too dry.

Serve with a little grated fresh Parmesan to taste.

Drink suggestion Try a dry, fresh and slightly acidic white wine, such as a Gavi.

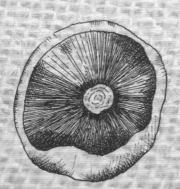

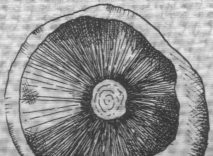

Risotto puttanesca

My friend Rob Little passed this recipe on to me. Rob lives on a narrow boat called *Scarlet*, so he knows a thing or two about cooking on a two-ring gas burner. Puttanesca sauce is perhaps more traditionally associated with spaghetti, but I think Rob was just working with whatever he had in his galley when he came up with this. Notice the 3:1 water to rice ratio – essential if you want to end up with a deliciously silky risotto.

Heat the oil in a large saucepan, add the garlic and cook for a minute or two, stirring and taking care not to burn it. Throw in the rice and give it a good stir to coat the grains in the garlicky oil. Pour in the glass of wine and stir again.

Add the anchovies, olives, capers and tomatoes. Turn the heat down to a gentle simmer. As the liquid is absorbed, stir in a little of the warm stock. When that is absorbed, add a little more, and stir again.

Repeat a few times until all the liquid is absorbed. When adding the last of the stock, stir in most of the Parmesan at the same time, keeping aside a little to garnish.

Season to taste and garnish with the remaining Parmesan.

Serve in deep-sided plates.

Drink suggestion Something crisp, fresh, dry and white, ideally from Sicily. If you can lay your hands on one, an Etna Bianco would be good. Otherwise an Albariño would be fine.

Ingredients Serves 4

- A glug of olive oil
- 4 cloves of garlic, crushed
- 300ml risotto rice (ideally Arborio)
- 1 glass of dry white wine (*not* optional!)
- 1 small tin of anchovies
- A handful of pitted black olives, roughly chopped
- A handful of capers
- A handful of sun-dried tomatoes, roughly chopped
- 900ml chicken or fish stock
- A handful of grated Parmesan cheese
- Sea salt & fresh ground black pepper

Equipment

Large saucepan, grater (if you're grating fresh cheese)

Ingredients Serves 4

- ○ 225g basmati rice
- ○ 1 star anise
- ○ 6 whole black peppercorns
- ○ 1 bay leaf
- ○ Sea salt
- ○ 450ml water
- ○ Olive oil
- ○ ½ small black pudding ring, skin removed, chopped into 1cm chunks
- ○ 4 large flat mushrooms, chopped
- ○ 4 smoked mackerel fillets (skin removed)
- ○ 12 cherry tomatoes, halved
- ○ Fresh basil leaves or flat leaf parsley to garnish

Equipment

Measuring jug, saucepan with lid, clean tea towel. sharp knife, non-stick frying pan

Perfect rice with smoked mackerel and black pudding

This one uses my foolproof "perfect rice" recipe and gives it an extra kick. Smoked mackerel is brilliantly versatile. Usually vacuum-packed, it keeps well in the coolbox and is just right for taking on a camping trip. In this dish, packed with gutsy flavours, the aromatic fish sits really well with the crisp, earthy black pudding.

Prepare the rice by placing it in a saucepan with the star anise, peppercorns and bay leaf. Add a pinch of sea salt and the water – use the measuring jug to make sure you've got exactly twice as much water as rice. Cover the pan with a lid and bring the liquid to the boil. Reduce to a low heat and leave to simmer very gently for 15 minutes.

Remove the lid from the saucepan and stir the rice gently with a fork. You will see that the majority of the liquid has been absorbed.

Fold the tea towel in half and place it over the pan. Place the lid back on, and press into place to give a tight fit. Fold the hanging corners of the tea towel onto the pan lid to stop them catching fire. Continue to simmer over a very low heat for another 5 minutes.

Turn off the heat and leave the pan to stand, unopened.

Next, fry the chopped black pudding in a drop of olive oil over a moderate flame. As the black pudding starts to crisp up, add the chopped mushrooms to the pan. Flake the mackerel fillets into the pan and stir just long enough to warm them through.

Add the mixture to the cooked rice and fork through a drizzle of olive oil.

Garnish with halved cherry tomatoes and ripped basil leaves or flat leaf parsley.

Drink suggestion Try a straightforward Chardonnay, from the Ardèche perhaps – a little oak should be fine, but avoid the heavy Aussie Chardonnays. Otherwise, a generic white Burgundy or Mâcon would be good; a red would be a mistake with smoked mackerel.

Basic couscous and beyond

Drink suggestion
It will set you back a few
pounds, but a Château Musar
red from Lebanon is a great
match for couscous. Or try
Alain Graillot's Syrah Tandem
from Morocco, if you can
track it down.

OK, the first of these isn't even an actual recipe. It basically
involves following the instructions – "add boiling water" –
on the side of a packet! However couscous, a staple of North
African cuisine, makes for a simple and (very) quick rice
substitute, and is great when it comes to saving gas. It also
absorbs flavours quickly, so whatever you introduce during
the soaking stage will give amazing results.

It's the elaborations on the basic recipe that get really
interesting. The spicy mushroom couscous, in particular, is a
real winner. It works with lamb, it works with fish, and it's out
of this world with marinated king prawns.

Basic couscous

Ingredients Serves 4
- 225g dried couscous
- 1 vegetable stock cube or
  1 tsp of bouillon powder
- 1 ltr boiling water
- A knob of butter
- Sea salt & fresh ground
  black pepper

Equipment
Mixing bowl, kettle
or saucepan

Place the couscous in a mixing bowl with the crumbled
stock cube or bouillon powder and add the water. It saves
gas to boil water in a kettle, but you can use a saucepan.

Leave the couscous to soak until all the stock has been
absorbed. Fork the knob of butter through before serving.
Season to taste.

It's that simple!

Spicy couscous

Toast the cumin and coriander seeds in a dry pan for a couple of minutes over a hot flame. Allow to cool a little, then grind them in a pestle and mortar.

Heat a little olive oil in the same pan and fry the chopped onion for 5 minutes. Add the ground spices and chopped chilli, stir well and cook for a further 3 or 4 minutes.

Throw in the sugar and the tablespoon of vinegar. Take care not to inhale the vinegar vapour, or you'll be coughing like a good 'un!

Add 225g of couscous and follow the "basic recipe" opposite, not forgetting the knob of butter forked through at the end.

Spicy mushroom couscous

Heat a couple of tablespoons of olive oil in a non-stick, high-sided frying pan. Add the chopped onion, garlic and chilli. Cook for 4 or 5 minutes, then add the chopped mushrooms.

While the onion and mushrooms are cooking, crush the fennel, cumin and coriander seeds together in a pestle and mortar. (I find it's easier if you crush the fennel and cumin seeds first and then add the coriander seeds.) Once the onion has begun to take on a little colour, stir in the crushed spices.

Add the sugar and the sherry vinegar and stir (don't inhale the vinegar vapour!).

Turn down the gas and add the couscous, stirring well and ensuring that the grains are well coated with the contents of the pan. Pour in the vegetable stock and stir through on a very low heat until the couscous has absorbed the liquid. Fork through the large knob of butter and serve hot with whatever you've got to hand.

Ingredients Serves 4

- ½ tsp cumin seeds
- 2 tsp coriander seeds
- Olive oil
- 1 onion, finely chopped
- ½ dried chilli, de-seeded and chopped
- ½ tsp sugar
- 1 tbsp white wine vinegar

Equipment

Non-stick frying pan, pestle and mortar, sharp knife, mixing bowl, kettle or saucepan

Ingredients Serves 4

- Olive oil
- 1 onion, finely chopped
- 2 cloves of garlic, finely chopped
- ½ fresh chilli, de-seeded and finely chopped
- 30g mushrooms, chopped
- 1 dessertspoon fennel seeds
- 1 tsp cumin seeds
- 1 tbsp coriander seeds
- 1 tsp sugar
- 1 tbsp sherry vinegar
- 225g dried couscous
- 500ml vegetable stock
- A large knob of butter

Equipment

Non-stick, high-sided frying pan, sharp knife, pestle and mortar, mixing bowl, kettle or saucepan

Pasta

PASTA REALLY IS the camper's friend. It's incredibly versatile, coming in so many shapes and sizes, and it's cheap and tasty and takes just minutes to prepare. Kids love it, adults love it – you can't go wrong. If you're not in the mood to cook a whole meal, you could just eat a bowl of pasta drizzled with butter, salt and black pepper or, better still, stir in a little fresh pesto. The recipes here are slightly more elaborate, however, ranging from a comforting spag bol to a cook-to-impress lobster feast. As for whether to use fresh or dried pasta, the jury's out. The fresh stuff certainly saves on cooking time and gas, but I'm not convinced that it tastes any better than dried. So use whatever you have!

Spaghetti Bolognese

Ingredients Serves 4

- Olive oil
- 1 onion, finely chopped
- 2 cloves of garlic, finely chopped
- 1 tsp paprika
- 500g minced beef
- Sea salt & fresh ground black pepper
- 1 tbsp plain flour
- 1 beef stock cube
- 1 tin of tomatoes
- 2 tsp tomato purée
- A pinch of dried oregano
- A good dash of Henderson's Yorkshire Relish (Worcester sauce will do)
- 400g spaghetti
- Grated Parmesan cheese

Equipment

Two large saucepans with lids, sharp knife, sieve or colander

It's called Bollywolly in our house – what do *you* call it? I was a little dubious about including my Bolognese recipe here. It is a regular in the Guyrope Gourmet camp kitchen, and so from that point of view makes sense, but I fear that once the secret is out, my kids will no longer be able to tell me that I make the best Bollywolly in the world!

Heat a good glug of olive oil in a large saucepan and cook the chopped onion. After 5 minutes throw in the chopped garlic and cook until the onion turns golden brown. Add the paprika and stir, and then add the minced beef, a good pinch of sea salt and a grind of fresh black pepper.

Cook until the meat has turned brown, and then add the flour and crumble in the stock cube. Stir the flour into the meat and cook for a couple of minutes, making sure it doesn't stick on the bottom of the pan.

Add the tin of tomatoes to the pan. Half-fill the empty tin with water and add that to the pan too. Stir well.

Add the tomato purée, dried oregano and Henderson's Relish, stir, and allow to simmer gently with the lid on. The Bolognese sauce will need to cook for at least 40 minutes (it gets better the longer you leave it).

While the sauce is cooking, bring a large pan of salted water to the boil. Cook the spaghetti according to the instructions on the packet.

When it's cooked, drain the spaghetti and serve it on warm plates topped with the flavourful sauce and sprinkled with grated Parmesan.

Drink suggestion Serve with a full-bodied red wine. A Barolo would be ideal.

- 1 fresh lobster (about 600g)
- Table salt, if required, for cooking
- 8 ripe plum tomatoes, peeled and chopped
- Olive oil
- 1 large onion, finely chopped
- 1 clove of garlic, finely chopped
- Sea salt & fresh ground black pepper
- Grated zest and juice of ½ lemon
- 250g linguini

Equipment

Large stockpot with lid (if you're cooking your own lobster), large bowl, saucepan with lid, grater, saucepan, sharp knife, chopping board, sieve or colander

Lobster with linguini and tomato sauce

Cooking a fresh lobster is an unforgettable Guyrope Gourmet experience. A live lobster has a beautiful blue hue to its shell, and the transformation, through the cooking process, to the familiar bright orange always amazes me. You can use a pre-cooked lobster from the fishmonger if you don't fancy cooking your own, or if you can't get hold of a live one, but be sure to buy a beast that was cooked the day you bought it.

Though it's not as complicated as it might sound, you'll need a bit of time for this recipe – the secret to a good tomato sauce is that it needs at least half an hour to cook.

Using a live lobster will always guarantee that it's fresh. Where possible, I boil mine in seawater, but if the sea is too far away then you can use ordinary water with table salt. You'll need about 160g of salt to 5 litres of water.

Bring the salted water to the boil in a large stockpot. Place the lobster, head first, into the pan and put the lid on. Hold the lid down for the first few seconds as the lobster may wriggle about (this is why some people might choose to buy a cooked lobster in the first place...). A 600g lobster will need 15 minutes in the pan. You don't need to boil it vigorously; a medium simmer will do nicely. Once the lobster is cooked, remove it to a plate and let it cool.

You could at this stage snap off the lobster's legs and break them up with your fingers, ready to be thrown in with the tomato sauce. They'll add some delicious flavour.

Cut a small "X" on the bottom of each tomato, place them in a large bowl and cover with boiling water. Allow them to stand until the skins come away, then remove the tomatoes from the bowl, allow them to cool and then peel and roughly chop them.

Heat a good glug of olive oil in a saucepan and cook the chopped onion gently for 10 minutes. Add the chopped garlic, chopped tomatoes and the legs from the lobster. Season well, stir and simmer gently with the lid on for 20 minutes or so. Remove the lid, fish out the lobster legs and add the lemon zest. Replace the lid and simmer for a further 10 minutes.

Cook the linguini according to the instructions on the packet.

Continues overleaf

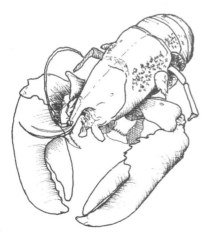

Remove the tail and claws from the lobster. You could either peel off the tail as if it were a giant prawn, which is a bit of a task or, more easily and quickly, cut the tail in half lengthwise using a sharp knife. To do this, place the tail underside down on a chopping board and insert the point of the knife through the shell at one end. With one hand on the knife handle and the other over the back of the blade, anchor the point on the chopping board and press the blade down through the shell lengthwise. You will then be able to remove the meat from the two halves. Crack the claws open with the back of the knife and tease out the meat.

Plate the cooked linguini, dress with tomato sauce and top with sliced lobster. A squeeze of the lemon will finish it off. If you are using a pre-cooked lobster, just slice it thinly – the heat from the sauce will soon warm it through.

Drink suggestion Lobster deserves a classy white wine – a white Burgundy, a dryish Riesling, or a fine Albariño all go well.

Spaghetti mare azzuro

Thanks to my pal Rob for this one. Rob's a great one for Italian food – if the amount of time he spent in the much-missed Spaccanapoli restaurant on Dean Street in London is anything to go by. Try his fishy pasta dish, made with a simple tin of sardines – it's easy, quick and tasty. A winner all round!

Cut a small "X" on the bottom of each tomato, chuck them in a bowl and cover with boiling water. Let them stand for a while, then remove from the water, allow to cool and peel off the skins.

Meanwhile, boil a large pan of water for the spaghetti (put a lid on the pan – it will boil more quickly and saves gas).

Rougly chop the peeled tomatoes, garlic and chillies. Fry gently in a little olive oil.

Cook the pasta according to the instructions on the packet.

Remove the sardines from the tin, split them and remove the backbones, and break the fish into large chunks. When the pasta is nearly ready, add the broken sardines to the tomato sauce. You just want to heat the fish through, so you're only looking at 2 or 3 minutes. Don't stir the sauce too much, or the fish will break up.

Drain the pasta, douse with a glug of olive oil and plate it up.

Pour the sauce over the pasta, and sprinkle with plenty of finely chopped fresh flat leaf parsley.

Drink suggestion A dry rosé – a Spanish Rosado from the Tempranillo grape would do nicely.

Ingredients Serves 2

- 10 plump cherry tomatoes
- 2 cloves of garlic
- 1 red chilli (2 if you're brave)
- Olive oil
- 250g spaghetti
- 1 tin of sardines
- Fresh flat leaf parsley, finely chopped

Equipment

Large bowl, large saucepan with lid, non-stick frying pan, sieve or colander

Smoky bonfire pasta

Ingredients Serves 4

- Olive oil
- 12 rashers of smoked streaky bacon
- 3 cloves of garlic, chopped
- 1 sprig of fresh thyme
- 1 tsp paprika
- ½ tsp smoked paprika
- 8 tomatoes (the size and colour of snooker balls), halved
- Pasta of your choice
- Salt
- A lump of Applewood smoked Cheddar, grated

Equipment

Large frying pan, grater, large saucepan, sieve or colander

Drink suggestion

A good Beaujolais such as a Morgon or a Beaujolais Villages should go well, but for a real treat you could enjoy a smoky, peaty single malt from Islay as a digestif.

As winter spreads its chilly cloak across the land and the final sunset of autumn casts a golden glow over the campsite, the thoughts of the Guyrope Gourmet turn to warmer clothes and warming dishes. This recipe for smoky bonfire pasta was first described to me by fellow camper and dear friend Rob. I love his description of "quality" smoked bacon, which truly demonstrates an appreciation of good food: "Really good smoked bacon should have yellow fat approaching the colour of straw, the meat should be more purple than pink, it should be dry to the touch and it should make your car smell like a garden in November. Someone's burning autumn leaves." Smoky bonfire pasta has become a firm favourite at home as well as in the tent. But don't eat it while wearing a white shirt!

Lay out the bacon in a large frying pan, with just a splash of olive oil. Cook over a low heat until the bacon turns crispy, with the fat the colour of amber. Remove the rashers from the pan and allow them to cool.

Add the chopped garlic to the pan and cook gently for 2 or 3 minutes. As soon as the garlic begins to colour, add the thyme and both types of paprika. Grate the halved tomatoes in to the pan, cut-side on the grater, leaving the skin behind. Stir the tomatoes through to make a rich vermilion sauce.

Bring a large saucepan of salted water to the boil and cook the pasta according to the instructions on the packet. Keep simmering the sauce gently.

When the pasta is nearly ready, snap the cooked bacon into small pieces, add it to the tomato sauce and stir until the bacon is heated through.

Drain the pasta and plate it up, cover with the sauce and top it all with a generous amount of grated cheese.

Spaghetti with oak roast salmon, lemon and basil

I was looking for a variation on spaghetti carbonara when I came up with this idea. The sauce is really quick to prepare and is practically done in the time it takes to cook your spaghetti. Oak roast salmon, which is first brined and then roasted over oak shavings at a high temperature, has a delightfully smoky, firm flesh that's easy to flake into salads or pasta. And it usually comes vacuum packed, which makes it ideal for storing in the coolbox.

Put a large pan of salted water on to boil for the pasta. While the water is coming to the boil, flake the salmon into a bowl, but try not to break it up too much.

Cook the pasta in the boiling water according to the instructions on the packet.

While the pasta is cooking, add the capers and the lemon zest to the flaked salmon, together with the olive oil. Squeeze in the juice from half the lemon, add a little sea salt and black pepper to taste and throw in the ripped basil. Stir gently with a fork and set to one side.

Drain the pasta and place in a bowl, then add the salmon dressing and fork through.

Drink suggestion Salmon, pasta, basil and lemon? Just pick your favourite dry white!

Ingredients Serves 2

- 200g oak roast salmon, flaked
- 200g spaghetti
- 1 tsp capers
- Grated zest & juice of a lemon
- A decent glug of good olive oil – around 5 tbsp, if you're measuring
- Sea salt & fresh ground black pepper
- A handful of ripped basil leaves

Equipment

Large saucepan, mixing bowl, sieve or colander

Linguini "salad" with rocket, toasted garlic and pine nuts

Ingredients Serves 2

- A glug of olive oil
- 4 garlic cloves, chopped
- 50g pine nuts
- 250g linguini
- Sea salt & fresh ground black pepper
- 8 fresh basil leaves, ripped
- A bag of rocket leaves
- 4 or 5 sun-dried tomatoes, finely chopped
- Shaved Parmesan

Equipment

Saucepan, non-stick frying pan, kitchen paper, large bowl, sieve or colander

There's something about warm pasta and fresh wilting rocket leaves that I really enjoy. I think it's the peppery bite of the leaves that does it and, when you add the flavours of toasted garlic, the odd pine nut and a few sun-dried tomatoes, this dish really starts to soar.

Put a pan of salted water on to boil for the pasta.

Heat a tiny glug of olive oil in a non-stick frying pan and add the chopped garlic. Cook gently until the garlic turns golden brown, but be careful not to burn it. Turn out onto a plate and set aside.

Give the frying pan a quick wipe with kitchen paper and toast the pine nuts in the dry pan over a moderate heat. Shake from time to time until the nuts darken, but again, don't overdo it. Set the nuts aside with the garlic.

Add the pasta to the boiling water and cook according to the instructions on the packet. When cooked, drain thoroughly and place in a bowl. Season well.

Scatter the pasta with the ripped basil leaves and a handful of the rocket and turn with a couple of forks. The heat from the pasta will wilt the leaves and bring out the flavour of the fresh basil. It will smell wonderful!

Next, scatter the garlic and pine nuts over the pasta, together with the chopped sun-dried tomatoes and a twist of black pepper for good measure. Throw another handful of rocket on top and drizzle with a little olive oil from the jar of sun-dried tomatoes. Top with shavings of good Parmesan.

Drink suggestion Enjoy with a crisp white wine. A Sauvignon Blanc, perhaps.

Fish & Seafood

I HAVE ALWAYS LOVED wet fish displays, and have marvelled since childhood at the ice-caked jigsaws of deep-sea creatures piled high on the fishmonger's slab. I find it very difficult to pass a fishmonger without popping in to buy something, especially when I'm camping, because – as a rule – fish is so easy to cook. Prepping can be a messy business, though, and sometimes a challenge on a campsite, but a fishmonger will always be happy to get the ball rolling for you, cleaning, de-scaling and removing the guts – and even the head if you're a bit squeamish.

Cooking and eating fresh shellfish in the open air is a particular treat, whether you're harvesting your own or getting your supplies from the local fishmonger. And while shellfish adds a touch of class to any camping meal, it can actually be a little easier to prepare than fish – and is surprisingly simple to cook. Always make sure that you eat shellfish on the day you get it, though, and give it a good rinse in cold water to get rid of any grit before cooking.

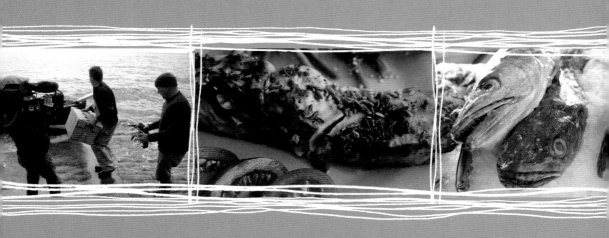

Grilled sardines

Ingredients

Use 2 or 3 fish per person

- Sardines (gutted and cleaned is best)
- Rock salt
- Lemons

Equipment

A barbecue. If you're cooking on an open fire, be sure to cook over the embers and not on a roaring flame.

The aroma of freshly grilled sardines always transports me to a *chiringuito* on a sandy Spanish beach. Seasoned with rock salt and lemon juice, the humble sardine is one of my favourite fish, and because they're naturally oily, they're ideal for the barbecue or an impromptu campfire.

You can get away with barbecuing sardines whole, but you'll need to take a little care when eating them so as not to take a bite of the less than palatable insides. Ideally I'd recommend gutting and cleaning the fish first (you can ask the fishmonger to do this – it's a bit messy and not much fun on a campsite!).

Set up your barbecue, and wait until the charcoal has turned grey before cooking. Place the sardines on a grill over the coals and cook for 3 or 4 minutes on each side. Remove to a plate, and dress with a pinch of rock salt and freshly squeezed lemon juice.

Eat the sardines with your fingers, starting at the tail end and working your way towards the head. That way you can simply slide the flesh off between your teeth, leaving the spine and the rest of the bones intact.

Drink suggestion If you want to avoid a horrible metallic clash, steer clear of assertive whites like Sauvignon Blancs. A dry rosé from Portugal or Provence, or a Spanish Rosado, will taste much better.

Salt and pepper squid

Ingredients Serves 6

- Vegetable oil for deep-frying
- 400g fresh or frozen squid
- A cup of plain flour
- Around 1 dessertspoon fresh ground black pepper
- Lots of flaked sea salt
- Lemon for squirting!

Equipment

Large saucepan or wok for deep-frying, tea towel, sharp knife, lots of kitchen paper, slotted spoon, bowl

Good on its own as a starter – and great with crusty bread and a cold beer as a light lunch – this dish is unbelievably easy to cook, but it does take some preparation. The trick to getting the best results is to make sure you dry the squid thoroughly, and the real secret is to dry it well when it's whole and then again after chopping. It's a bit faffy, for sure, but well worth the effort (and plenty of kitchen paper helps). If you're really pushed for time you could short-cut the drying process, but it'll end up a bit claggy. (Claggy and faffy – these are bona fide cooking terms, honest!)

You can use frozen or fresh squid. If you're buying fresh, ask the fishmonger to prepare it for you; they'll need to remove the purple outer skin and the clear spine from inside the body.

Pour about 5cm of vegetable oil into a large saucepan ready for deep-frying. If you've brought a wok along with you, all the better.

Dry the whole squid thoroughly, using a tea towel. If you're using the frozen variety sold in some supermarkets you'll find that the tentacles have already been cut away and are tucked up inside the body. You can squeeze the tentacles out once the squid has thawed.

Chop the squid into rings and, once again dry thoroughly, this time using kitchen paper. Put the flour into a bowl and grind in plenty of black pepper – a good dessertspoonful ought do the trick. Throw in five good pinches of flaked sea salt and mix in with your fingers.

Before you coat the squid with the seasoned flour, you need to make sure that the oil in the pan is hot enough for deep-frying. As my home economics teacher Mrs Walker used to say, "a good cook never fries 'til he sees the blue smoke rise!" When the oil is hot, toss the squid thoroughly through the seasoned flour, ensuring that each piece is well coated.

Carefully spoon the coated squid into the hot oil. It should effervesce immediately. Deep-fry for 3 or 4 minutes, and watch as the coating turns a lovely golden colour. Lift out with a slotted spoon into a bowl lined with kitchen paper. Let drain for a few seconds then remove the paper. Squeeze the juice of half a lemon over the squid just before serving.

Drink suggestion An ice-cold Mexican beer with a wedge of fresh lime in the neck. If you prefer wine, go for a crisp dry white – a Muscadet would be great.

Stuffed trout wrapped in maize leaves

Ingredients Serves 2

- ○ 2 fresh cobs of corn with leaves still attached
- ○ 2 bay leaves
- ○ 2 cloves of garlic, sliced
- ○ 4 large knobs of butter
- ○ A large bunch of fresh thyme
- ○ ½ lemon
- ○ 2 trout, cleaned and gutted
- ○ Sea salt & fresh ground black pepper

Equipment

A barbecue (or an open fire) and a couple of small wooden toothpicks

Drink suggestion

A light white or a dry rosé from anywhere in the world.

I rustled this one up while camping in the Redwoods in California. I was planning to propose to my girlfriend when we got to the coast and, in preparation, was now pulling out all the stops in trying to impress.

It's a really straightforward dish to cook over an open fire or on a barbecue. The only fiddly bit is wrapping the maize leaves around the trout to stop the skin burning. Once the fish is well wrapped, I pin the leaves in place with a couple of wooden toothpicks to stop them unravelling.

Fire up the barbie! Or, if you're lucky enough to be camping where open fires are permitted, build a fire.

Carefully peel off a couple of the outer leaves from each of the corn cobs, but make sure the yellow kernels are still covered – you don't want them burning over the fire. Put the corn on the barbie or the fire to cook, turning as necessary.

Stuff one bay leaf, half of the sliced garlic, a knob of butter, half of the thyme and a good wedge of lemon into one of the trout. Apply a good sprinkle of sea salt and a generous grind of black pepper to the outside of the fish. Do the same with the second fish.

Wrap the trout in the two leaves from the corn and pin them closed using wooden toothpicks. Place on the barbecue or fire, and cook for about 10 minutes on each side. The trout and the corn should be ready at about the same time.

Spread a knob of butter over the cooked corn on the cob, and enjoy with the stuffed trout.

Fish tagine

A tagine is an earthenware cooking pot with a conical lid. They're popular across the Middle East, where they're used in even the most basic of kitchens.

When camping, I use a high-sided frying pan with a lid as a more robust substitute for the terracotta pot. The end result is just as good, and the smell of fresh ground cumin wafting around the tent speaks of new Bedouin cuisine ... "New Bedouin cuisine" – now there's an idea!

Ingredients Serves 4

- 2 large skinned fillets of white fish (haddock, cod, whatever)
- ¾ tsp cumin seeds
- 1 tbsp coriander seeds
- 2 tsp fennel seeds
- 3 cloves of garlic
- Sea salt & fresh ground black pepper
- 1 heaped tsp paprika
- Olive oil
- 1 lemon
- 6 or 8 baby new potatoes or salad potatoes
- 1 onion
- 1 bulb of fennel
- 1 red pepper
- A handful of pitted olives (a mixture of black and green looks good)
- A handful of cherry tomatoes, halved
- 400ml bouillon/vegetable stock
- A small glass of white wine (optional)
- Fresh flat leaf parsley, chopped

Equipment

Sharp knife, bowl, pestle and mortar, saucepan, tagine or high-sided frying pan with a lid.

Cut the fish into large chunks and place in a bowl.

Grind the cumin, coriander and fennel seeds in a pestle and mortar, chuck in the whole garlic cloves, a pinch of sea salt, a grind of black pepper and the paprika. Grind into a chunky paste and add the olive oil and the juice of half the lemon. Give it all a good stir and pour it over the fish. Leave to marinate for as long as you can wait.

Heat a saucepan of water and parboil the potatoes, whole, for 5 or 6 minutes. Drain, allow to cool and cut into halves.

Halve the onion and slice thinly. Top and tail the bulb of fennel and finely chop.

Heat a glug of oil in a tagine or high-sided frying pan and cook the onion and fennel gently. While that is cooking, blacken a whole red pepper over a naked flame. Scrape off the skin, cut in half, remove the seeds and slice.

Once the onion has taken on a little colour, place the chunks of fish into the pan, and add the potatoes and sliced red pepper. Throw in the olives and the halved cherry tomatoes and pour in the rest of the marinade. Add the bouillon or stock, and pour in a small glass of white wine if you have one. Place the lid on the tagine or pan and simmer very gently for 20 minutes or so, until the fish is cooked.

Garnish with a generous handful of the flat leaf parsley.

Drink suggestion The assertive Middle Eastern flavours in this dish call for wine with a bit of character. Perhaps a Spanish white such as an Albariño or Godello, or a Soave from a good grower like Coffele or Pieropan.

Mussels with beer and coriander

Ingredients Serves 4
- 1kg fresh mussels, scraped, washed and de-bearded
- 2 tbsp olive oil
- 1 small red onion, finely chopped
- 1 tin of chopped tomatoes
- Sea salt & fresh ground black pepper
- 1 small "stubby" of lager (33cl)
- A good handful of fresh coriander, chopped

Equipment
Sharp knife, wok or large stockpot with a lid

This recipe was given to me by my pal Glyn. I think he came up with it himself, and I probably owe him a bottle of Cava for it. I was dining at Fish! in London's Borough Market a couple of years back and, emboldened by my third glass of Cava, I asked the waiter if the chef would be so kind as to knock me up some mussels cooked this way. To my pleasant surprise, he did – and he also came out to our table and informed me that it was so good he'd like to put it on the menu! By all means, said I, as he offered us a complimentary (fifth) glass of fizz.

Mussels should be easy to find if you're camping in Scotland, or near the coast. There is an old saying that you should only eat them when there's an "r" in the month, but this adage pre-dates the modern methods of farming rope-grown mussels. These are available all year round; most mussels you get in supermarkets and fishmongers are of the rope-grown variety.

Check over your mussels, and discard any open ones that don't close when tapped with a knife.

Heat the olive oil in a wok or large stockpot and cook the chopped onion over a moderate heat until softened. Add the scraped, washed and de-bearded mussels and the chopped tomatoes and give it all a stir. Add the salt and pepper and pour in the lager. Place a lid on the pot and let it simmer for 3 or 4 minutes, depending on how well cooked you like your mussels.

Add the chopped coriander to the pan once it is removed from the heat. Let stand for a minute before serving, and discard any mussels that didn't open after cooking.

Drink suggestion Cava, naturally! Failing that, a glass of the same beer that the mussels were simmered in.

Fish chowder

Ingredients Serves 2

- 2 large leeks, chopped
- A large knob of butter
- 6 or 8 whole black peppercorns (optional)
- Salt
- ¼ tsp white pepper
- 1 tbsp plain flour
- 500g waxy potatoes, such as Charlottes, peeled and diced
- 500ml fish stock – made from a stock cube is fine
- 250ml full-fat milk
- 400g skinned fillets of white fish, such as coley, cod or haddock, cut into large pieces
- 3 tbsp sweetcorn (which is most of a small tin)
- 50ml double cream
- Fresh chives, chopped

Equipment

A large saucepan

More filling than a soup and too delicate to be called a stew, chowders are a speciality of New England. This is a simplified version of the many elaborate chowders I devoured during my stay in New Hampshire back in the 1990s. If you're camping by the coast you could throw in a handful of cooked peeled shrimp or a few fresh cockles, if you like but, whatever you do, be sure to use whole (full-fat) milk – it just doesn't work with semi-skimmed. Enjoy with chunks of bread.

Trim the green tops and the roots from the leeks, cut in half lengthwise and chop roughly. Melt the butter in a large saucepan and add the chopped leeks and the whole peppercorns (if you have them). Cook for about 5 minutes until the leeks have softened.

Add a pinch of salt and the white pepper together with the flour. Stir well and cook for a couple of minutes. Don't worry if the mixture starts to stick to the bottom of the pan – it will loosen up as soon as you add the stock.

Throw in the diced potatoes and stir. Add the fish stock a little at a time, and then the milk. Simmer gently for 10 or 15 minutes, until the potatoes begin to soften.

Remove the pan from the heat. Carefully place the pieces of fish into the pan along with the sweetcorn. Bring back to a gentle simmer, but do not boil or the fish will break up. Cook gently for a further 5 minutes.

Gently stir in the double cream just before serving. Top with chopped fresh chives.

Drink suggestion Any light dry white (not too sharp) would go well with this dish.

Marinated tuna steaks

Fresh tuna is not cheap, but it does make for a splendid treat every now and again. I like mine served with a crunchy green salad and a couple of spoonfuls of fresh tomato salsa. A slice of good brown toast would round it off nicely.

Combine the chilli, lime juice and sweet chilli dipping sauce in a mixing bowl, and add a pinch of sea salt and plenty of ground black pepper. Pour over the tuna steaks and leave to steep while you prepare a fresh green salad and the tomato salsa (see p64).

Heat a dry griddle pan over a high flame to very hot and flick a drop of the marinade onto the pan. If it sizzles and steams, then the pan is ready for the fish. Depending on the thickness of the tuna steaks, cook for no more than 1½ minutes on each side. This will leave a nice stripe of pink through the middle of your steak.

Drink suggestion An unoaked white or a light red.

Ingredients Serves 2

- 1 small green chilli, de-seeded and finely chopped
- Juice of a lime
- 1 tbsp sweet chilli dipping sauce
- Sea salt & fresh ground black pepper
- 2 small tuna steaks (1 per person)

Equipment
Mixing bowl, griddle pan, sharp knife

Salmon with honey and fennel seeds

A versatile fish if ever there was one, salmon. Until the age of about nine, I only ever saw it in a tin. The price of fresh salmon placed it firmly beyond the means of many. Since the advent of salmon farming, however, it has become much more affordable and, as a fresh fish, it's pretty hard to beat. A simple treatment of olive oil, lime juice and a few other bits and pieces renders it fine camping fare – delicious with a side dish of green beans and toasted sesame seeds (see p182). Most fishmongers will sell salmon fillets in single portions. Skin on or skin off, it doesn't really matter – it just alters the cooking time a little. If you can only find a large fillet, make sure you cut it into portions before marinading, as this will give the flavours a chance to permeate.

Place the salmon fillets in a shallow dish and drizzle with the lime juice, a little olive oil, the honey and a pinch of sea salt. Add a grind of fresh black pepper, the fennel seeds and the sliced garlic. Roll the fish around in the bowl and let it stand for as long as you can wait. Half an hour would be good, but who's timing?

Place the fillets (skin side down, if they have skin) in a hot non-stick frying pan. Cook for 5 minutes (4 if your fish is skinless) then turn over and brown the top for about 2 minutes. You can throw in the rest of the marinade at this point, if you like, and enjoy the sizzle.

Once the fish is cooked, remove any skin and serve.

Drink suggestion An Australian Clare Valley Riesling would be the ideal accompaniment to this dish.

Ingredients Serves 2

- 200g salmon fillets
- Juice of a lime
- Olive oil
- 1 tsp clear honey
- Sea salt & fresh ground black pepper
- 1 tsp fennel seeds
- 1 clove of garlic, sliced

Equipment

Shallow dish, non-stick frying pan

Deep-fried nightfish

Ingredients Serves 2
- Whitebait (a couple of good handfuls)
- Plain flour
- Sea salt & fresh ground black pepper
- Olive oil

Equipment
Saucepan for deep-frying, slotted spoon, kitchen paper

Deep-fried nightfish may well be the most romantic meal I've ever cooked. The first time I prepared it, my girlfriend (now wife!) had accepted my proposal of marriage an hour or so before, as the sun went down over the Pacific Ocean. Anne-Marie and I were camping on Usal Beach in Sinkyone State Park, a wilderness park on the lost coast of northern California, when a stranger showed up with a triangular fishing net. "I'm looking for nightfish," he declared. "They follow the dayfish." It turns out that this chap — one John Maybury, of Fort Bragg, California — was fishing for grunion, a small fish not dissimilar to the whitebait that is so common in British waters. I traded a handful of his catch for a couple of my cold beers. I guess you could say that it was the greatest catch of my life!

Toss the whitebait in seasoned flour. Deep-fry in a saucepan of hot olive oil until crispy. Remove with a slotted spoon onto sheets of kitchen paper to drain.

Drink suggestion A cold beer — what else? If there's no cold beer to hand, try a dry rosé. A Spanish Rosado would be ideal.

Marinated king prawns

I sometimes cheat and bring a bag of frozen king prawns with me on a camping trip. By the time I cook them, usually the next day, they'll have played their part in cooling my wine and will be well on their way to thawing out. I use the shell-on variety, but that's only because I like getting my fingers sticky when it comes to tucking in! You can use peeled prawns if you prefer. Either way, they taste great served with spicy couscous (see p111) or perfect rice (p96).

Mix all the ingredients together in a bowl and leave to marinade for at least half an hour. (You can use this time to prepare either the rice or couscous.)

When you're ready to eat, throw the lot into a non-stick frying pan and fry over a high heat for 4 or 5 minutes, stirring well with a wooden spoon. The prawns turn pink as they cook and the marinade will start to caramelise. Turn out onto a bed of rice or couscous and tuck in.

Drink suggestion A dry, not overly assertive white, like a Verdicchio from Italy or a Verdejo Rueda from Spain, will complement the herbs and spices in this dish.

Ingredients Serves 4

- 16 uncooked shell-on king prawns (more if you're hungry)
- 4 tbsp olive oil
- Juice of a lime
- 1 clove of garlic, finely chopped
- ¼ dried red chilli, chopped
- Sea salt & fresh ground black pepper
- 1 tsp paprika
- A good handful of chopped fresh coriander
- A dash of soy sauce (but don't get hung up about it if you forgot to pack it!)

Equipment
Bowl, non-stick frying pan, wooden spoon

Poached sea bass

Ingredients Serves 2

- A whole sea bass, cleaned and gutted (ask the fishmonger to do this – it'll save a lot of mess back on the campsite)
- 1 carrot
- ½ bulb of fennel
- A knob of butter
- Sea salt & fresh ground black pepper
- A little water

Equipment

Kitchen foil, sharp knife, barbecue or grill

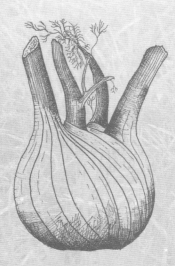

Poaching really brings out the delicate flavours of fish. My "fish kettle" started life as a sterilising bath for surgical instruments. I spotted it on a stall at a flea market and instantly saw its potential. You don't really need a fish kettle, though – or a sterilising bath – as you can get a similar result by wrapping the fish in a well-sealed, strong foil parcel and cooking it over a barbecue.

Place the fish on a large double sheet of kitchen foil. Peel and slice the carrot, and chop the fennel. Place a few of the vegetables and the knob of butter in the body cavity of the fish and dot a few veg around the fish too.

Season the fish with sea salt and black pepper and close the foil around it to form a loose-fitting "bag". Leave plenty of room in there; this will allow the fish to steam in its juices.

Pour in a little water before you seal the bag. Make sure the foil is well sealed all around – you don't want any of the steam to escape while cooking.

Cook the fish parcel over a barbecue or on a grill over your camping stove on a moderate heat for about 10 minutes. Be careful when opening the parcel – the steam will be hot!

Drink suggestion A fine but not overly assertive dry white – perhaps a Chablis, an Alsace Pinot Blanc or a Riesling.

Scallops wrapped in pancetta

I'm delighted and rather proud to say that I have cooked this dish for a National Seafood Chef of the Year. Mr Rob Green of the splendid Green's Bistro in Whitby very kindly agreed to come along and sample my food for a short TV programme we were making for the BBC. I was looking for a starter to impress and served this on a bed of rocket with shaved Parmesan. Rob thought it was spot on. He called me a genius with a camp stove. I do like Rob Green!

Remove the corals (the orange, tongue-like appendages) from the scallops, and discard them. This makes it easier to do the next bit.

Wrap each scallop in a slice of pancetta and impale each one on two wooden skewers (using two skewers makes it easier to turn the scallop over when cooking).

Drizzle the scallops lightly with olive oil and cook on a hot griddle pan for 2 minutes on each side.

Once cooked, serve the scallops on a bed of rocket with the shaved Parmesan and a drizzle of olive oil.

Drink suggestion A good dry – but not too dry – white with some body, such as a dry white Bordeaux or a Godello.

Ingredients Serves 2

- ○ 4 king scallops
- ○ 4 slices of pancetta
- ○ Good olive oil
- ○ A handful of rocket leaves
- ○ Shaved Parmesan

Equipment

Sharp knife, wooden skewers, griddle pan

Stuffed mackerel

Ingredients

Serves 2

- 2 mackerel
- 1 lemon, quartered
- A bunch of fresh coriander, chopped
- A bunch of flat leaf parsley, chopped
- Olive oil

Equipment

Sharp knife, barbecue

On a recent trip to Staithes on the North Yorkshire coast, I witnessed the skipper of a small boat gutting mackerel in a most unusual manner. He called it "fancy gutting" and I fancied a go. Sean had caught plenty, so he let me have a couple to try my hand at.

Despite its name, the "fancy" technique turned out to be as easy as it looked. The beauty of it is that, with the fish's belly left intact, the cavity is perfect for stuffing, making this a superb option for a barbecue. Some might choose to dish it up with a gooseberry sauce, but the Guyrope Gourmet would urge you to keep things simple and to let the lemon and fresh herb stuffing do its magic.

Gut the fish using the "fancy gutting" method:

- Using a sharp knife, make a small slit forward from the anus (which is on the underside of the fish just before the tail)
- Prise out a small loop of intestine from the slit and sever the intestine
- Make a cut around the fish's head at about a 45-degree angle
- Twist and pull the head and guts away from the body
- Rinse the fish under running water

Stuff the cavity of the fish with a wedge of lemon and a handful of fresh coriander and flat leaf parsley. Drizzle with olive oil and barbecue for 5 minutes on each side.

Drink suggestion Dry cider would counter the oily fish; otherwise try a white with good acidity, such as a Portuguese Alvarinho.

Fish Provençal

Ingredients Serves 2

- Olive oil
- 1 large onion, finely chopped
- 2 cloves of garlic, finely chopped
- 1 stick of celery, thinly sliced
- 1 red pepper, chopped
- 2 courgettes, thinly sliced
- 6 tomatoes, quartered, de-seeded and roughly chopped
- Sea salt & fresh ground black pepper
- A couple of fillets of any sort of fish you fancy – coley is good and cheap
- Fresh flat leaf parsley, chopped

Equipment

Sharp knife, high-sided frying pan, non-stick frying pan

This recipe, submitted to the Guyrope Gourmet website by fellow Trangia enthusiast, Sue Gardiner, is a cinch. I love the way she just flings it all together with little regard to stipulating quantities. Whether you add a bit too much of this, or not enough of the other, you just know it's going to taste great. The suggested quantities are mine, not Sue's. Follow them, or ignore them and guesstimate your own.

For the sauce, heat some olive oil in a high-sided frying pan and cook the onion, garlic and celery for a few minutes. Add the pepper and courgettes. Once the courgettes begin to soften, add the chopped tomatoes and season to taste. Let the sauce simmer slowly for at least 40 minutes.

Once the sauce has cooked, heat a little olive oil in a separate non-stick frying pan and fry your chosen fish. A couple of minutes on each side should do (it really depends on what fish you go for).

Serve the fish with the Provençal sauce and sprinkle with the chopped parsley.

Drink suggestion A crisp, dry white or a dry rosé.

Cockles with white wine and parsley

Cockles remind me of my very early childhood. I remember clambering over what seemed like huge mountains of empty shells around the back of the cockle sheds in Leigh-on-Sea, where I used to live. You don't always find them, but I do keep an eye out for cockles when we're camping near the sea; they're particularly good when given a simple treatment of white wine and fresh chopped parsley.

Melt the butter in a large, shallow frying pan and sauté the shallots. Turn up the heat, add the rinsed cockles and pour in the glass of wine. Season well and simmer until the shells have opened.

Remove from the heat and discard any unopened cockles. Garnish with the chopped flat leaf parsley.

Drink suggestion Enjoy with the white wine left over after cooking – and make sure it's as cold as possible.

Ingredients Serves 2

- ○ A knob of butter
- ○ 2 or 3 shallots, finely chopped
- ○ 500g live cockles, thoroughly rinsed to remove grit and mud
- ○ 1 large glass of white wine – a Muscadet would be good
- ○ Sea salt & fresh ground black pepper
- ○ A good handful of fresh flat leaf parsley, chopped

Equipment
Sharp knife, large frying pan

Meat & Poultry

I HAVE TO ADMIT THAT I find it hard to think about food without thinking about meat. As a carnivore, I get an almost primeval kick out of sitting around a campfire with a barbecued chicken leg or a juicy lamb chop in my hand. And I'm fascinated by the way geography comes into play, informing the meat's flavour. Saltmarsh-fed lamb, or Welsh spring lamb? Same animal, different taste. Even a simple sausage can be influenced by regional variations. The Cumberland, the Lincolnshire, the Oxford – they all have their differences. Try cooking any of the following recipes on a campsite, with local ingredients – and then try them again back at home. I bet you'll taste a difference.

Basic burgers

Ingredients Serves 4

- A knob of butter
- 1 large onion, peeled and grated
- 2 cloves garlic, very finely chopped
- 500g good-quality minced beef
- Sea salt & fresh ground black pepper

Equipment

Frying pan, grater, sharp knife, mixing bowl, tea towel, barbecue

It would be verging on rude not to include a burger recipe in a camping cookbook. You can buy them ready-made from any good butcher, of course, but there's something about creating your own that makes them taste so much better. If you use good beef, the only seasoning you'll need is a little salt and pepper.

After years of trying, I have finally discovered that the best way to build a decent burger is to use grated onion. No matter how fine I've tried to make it, chopped onion always ends up lumpy and makes the burger fall apart. Grating is the answer. Those onion tears will be tears of joy in the end. Cooking the onion first adds great flavour, and it also means that you won't be chewing on bits of raw onion as you tuck in.

Burgers are best cooked over a barbecue. You just don't get that wonderful smoky flavour if you fry them. But remember – never start cooking until the charcoal has turned grey.

Melt the knob of butter in the frying pan and throw in the grated onion. Simmer for 5 minutes, then add the chopped garlic. Cook until the onion turns a lovely golden brown. Remove from the heat and allow to cool.

Place the minced beef in a mixing bowl and season well with sea salt and ground black pepper. Rub the seasoning through the meat with your hands.

Add the cooked onion and garlic to the bowl and work it through so that it is evenly distributed through the meat.

Divide the mix into four and shape into balls about the size of billiard balls. Put them on a plate and cover with a tea towel.

Leave to stand while you fire up the barbecue.

Most barbecues are ready after about 30 minutes – but whatever you do, don't start cooking until the flames have died down and the coals have turned grey.

When you're ready to get going, take a ball of meat and squash it between your palms into a burger shape.

Barbecue for about 3 minutes on each side.

Moroccan lamb meatballs with fresh tomato sauce

From a financial point of view, my first visit to Morocco, back in the 1990s, was a disaster. Having been waylaid – on several occasions – in the souk, I came away laden with a load of old tut, tat and an armful of "gifts" that I never wanted to buy. In mitigation, I also came away with an appreciation for speedy, simple food and, above all, an insight into the wonder that is ground cumin, a key flavour in this glorious dish. I have recreated this from memory – not an inconsiderable feat, given the somewhat hedonistic approach I had to my travels in Morocco. It works particularly well with tabouleh (see p57).

You'll need very fine mince, so ask the butcher to put the lamb through the mincer a couple of times. The tomato sauce is easy; grating the tomatoes, instead of peeling and chopping them, makes for a much smoother texture.

Ingredients   Serves 4 – makes about 28 small meatballs

For the meatballs:
- ○ 1 tsp cumin seeds
- ○ 1 tbsp coriander seeds
- ○ 500g minced lamb
- ○ A pinch of paprika
- ○ Sea salt & fresh ground black pepper

For the tomato sauce:
- ○ A little olive oil
- ○ 1 clove of garlic, finely chopped
- ○ 6 tomatoes, halved
- ○ Sea salt & fresh ground black pepper
- ○ A handful of fresh flat leaf parsley, chopped

Equipment
Two non-stick frying pans, pestle and mortar, bowl, grater, sharp knife

First, make the meatballs. Toast the cumin and coriander seeds in a dry non-stick frying pan for a couple of minutes, keeping them on the move so they don't burn. Just marvel at that aroma! Remove the seeds from the pan and crush them to a powder using a pestle and mortar.

Place the minced lamb in a bowl together with the crushed spices, the paprika, a pinch of sea salt and a grind of fresh black pepper.

Using your fingertips, work the spices through the meat, mixing thoroughly. Make the meatballs by taking a pinch of the meat and rolling it between your palms to form a ball the size of a large marble. The mixture should make about 28 small meaballs. Set aside on a plate.

Heat a non-stick frying pan and cook the meatballs (you won't need any oil in the pan, as the fat will begin to come out of the meat). Keep moving the meatballs around in the pan to ensure they brown on all sides.

While the meatballs are cooking, prepare the tomato sauce. Place a drop of olive oil in a non-stick frying pan and add the chopped garlic. Once the garlic starts to cook, grate the halved tomatoes, cut-side on the grater, into the pan. Discard the skin, which will remain in your hand. Stir and season to taste as the grated tomatoes begin to thicken to a sauce. By the time the meatballs are cooked, the sauce will have thickened.

Take the meatballs and the sauce off the heat. Add a handful of chopped flat leaf parsley to the sauce and spoon it over the meatballs.

Drink suggestion A Rioja or any Spanish red based on the Tempranillo grape.

Pork stir fry

From a gas-saving perspective, stir fries are the ideal camping food as they take just a few minutes to cook. They take a little longer to prepare, but I think there is something rather therapeutic about chopping and prepping all the ingredients as you sit around in camp. The key to a good stir-fry is to make sure you have all the bits chopped and ready, as you need to throw them into the pan in fairly rapid succession. Once you start to fry, the whole thing should be done in about six minutes.

I always use button mushrooms for a stir fry. While they may lack the flavour of the larger field, or even chestnut, mushrooms, I find that using field mushrooms tends to turn the final result an unappetising grey as the spores are released in cooking.

Cut the pork loin chops into 2cm strips. Mix together the soy sauce, chopped ginger, sugar and lime juice in a large bowl and marinate the pork strips in the marinade while you are preparing the rest of the ingredients.

Warm the oil in a large wok or non-stick frying pan and cook the sliced onion until soft. After a couple of minutes, throw in the pork and the marinade. Keep the ingredients moving around in the pan using a wooden spoon.

Add the sliced mushrooms, spring onions and peppers, and stir well. Add a pinch of sea salt, a good grind of black pepper and the Chinese five spice. Throw in the beansprouts, stir well for another minute or so and serve.

Drink suggestion A not-too-expensive French Sauvignon should go well – try a Bordeaux Sauvignon or a Sauvignon de Touraine.

Ingredients Serves 2

- 2 pork loin chops
- 4 tbsp soy sauce
- 2cm fresh ginger, peeled and finely chopped
- ¾ tsp sugar
- Juice of 1 lime
- Vegetable oil for frying (use groundnut oil if you can find it)
- 1 small onion, finely sliced
- A handful of button mushrooms, finely sliced
- 6 or 8 spring onions, finely sliced
- 1 red pepper, de-seeded and sliced lengthwise
- 1 green pepper, de-seeded and sliced lengthwise
- Sea salt & fresh ground black pepper
- ½ tsp Chinese five spice
- A big handful of fresh beansprouts

Equipment

Sharp knife, large bowl, large wok or non-stick frying pan, wooden spoon

Dusted chicken breasts

Ingredients This will
make enough for 4 sandwiches

- ○ 2 chicken breasts
- ○ A couple of tbsp plain flour
- ○ Grated zest and juice of a lemon
- ○ A small bunch of fresh thyme, chopped
- ○ Sea salt & fresh ground black pepper
- ○ Olive oil

Equipment
Sharp knife, bowl, grater, griddle pan or heavy-based frying pan

This simple chicken dish goes well with a crisp green salad and a dollop of delicious mayonnaise for a cheeky chicken sandwich. It works best if you cut up the breast, rather than use a whole one – increasing the surface area of the meat allows the chicken to take on more of the flavour from the seasoned flour. Cutting the breasts into smaller strips also allows the coating to crisp up a bit more in the pan.

Slice each chicken breast into four or five pieces. Cut them diagonally so that your chicken strips are about 5cm long.

Place the flour into a bowl and grate in the lemon zest (keep the lemon, as you'll be needing a squeeze of the juice later). Remove the thyme leaves from the stalks, chop them roughly and add them to the flour. Throw in a pinch of sea salt and a good grind of black pepper. Mix thoroughly with a fork and toss the chicken in the flour, making sure that each piece is well dusted.

Place the griddle pan on the stove and, while it's warming up, spread the chicken out on a plate and drizzle with olive oil. (It's always best to oil the food rather than the pan if you are cooking on a griddle.) Once the griddle is hot, cook the chicken for 3 minutes on each side. When it's done, squeeze over the juice of half the lemon.

Drink suggestion Chicken with lemon suggests a crisp white, but thyme likes red wine best. A lightish young Rioja would be good and, for a white, a Soave.

Herby lamb cutlets

I've never been entirely sure as to what exactly constitutes a "cutlet". As far as I can see, it's basically a fancy way of describing a chop!

The combination of tender lamb, melting butter and fresh herbs makes this simple little number a favourite of mine. It's fantastic finger food, and perfect for the great outdoors.

Dust the lamb chops with a pinch of sea salt and a grind of black pepper and set aside while you prepare the herbs.

Remove the rosemary leaves from the stalk and chop them with the mint leaves. (Rosemary tends to be a bit woody, so be sure to chop it as finely as you can.) Combine the herbs with the butter and mix thoroughly with a fork.

Griddle or fry the chops in a very hot pan for a couple of minutes on each side. I like my lamb pink in the middle – you may want to cook yours for a little longer.

Remove the chops from the pan and spread each side with a smear of the herb butter.

Drink suggestion Red Bordeaux, the classic combination with lamb, would go well, but the rosemary and mint here would also suit a red from the Languedoc – perhaps a Corbières or Minervois. A red Rioja would be fine too.

Ingredients Serves 2
- 1 or 2 lamb chops per person (I guess it depends on the size and the price – and the appetites concerned!)
- Sea salt & fresh ground black pepper
- A sprig of fresh rosemary
- 12 fresh mint leaves
- A large knob of butter

Equipment
Sharp knife, griddle or non-stick frying pan

Medallions of wild venison with port and cherry sauce

Ingredients Serves 2

- A couple of knobs of butter
- A handful of fresh cherries, pitted and roughly chopped
- A small glass of port (about 100ml)
- ½ tsp sugar
- 250g loin of venison
- Fresh ground black pepper
- 220g baby leaf spinach

Equipment

Small saucepan with lid, non-stick frying pan

Despite the fancy-sounding name, this is a really simple dish that only takes twenty minutes or so to prepare. The fruit works beautifully with the venison, complementing the gamey flavour of the meat, and served with wilted spinach it's out of this world. Venison, for some reason, speaks to me of Christmas, but it is available all year round and a surprising number of butchers seem to stock it nowadays. It's a very lean meat, and comparable with lamb in price.

I once prepared this dish while camping in Savernake Forest in Wiltshire. The fact that the meat we were eating had grown and lived as a wild animal in that same forest made the occasion all the more special. I have to say I've not tasted a finer piece of venison since.

Melt a small knob of butter in a saucepan over a moderate heat. Throw in the pitted and chopped cherries, together with the port and the sugar. Simmer gently, covered, for 10 minutes. The cherries should soften but not lose their form.

While the cherries are simmering, melt another knob of butter in a non-stick frying pan and, once that has become hot, place the venison loin in the pan. It should be sizzling nicely as it goes in.

Depending how well done you like your meat, cook for about 4 or 5 minutes on each side for medium rare; 6 or 7 minutes on each side will see the meat well done. Once cooked, remove the meat from the pan and place on a plate to rest.

Pour the cherry mixture into the frying pan with the venison and simmer vigorously to reduce. This way, the juices from the meat aren't wasted and will add a good depth of flavour to the sauce. Cut the loin into 5mm slices, plate it up and drizzle it with the cherry and port sauce. Season to taste with ground black pepper.

To prepare the spinach, add just a tiny splash of water to a hot pan, throw in the spinach and stir – it will wilt in a matter of seconds.

Drink suggestion A Californian red Zinfandel or a South American Merlot should have enough fruit to match the sweetness here.

Spatchcocked poussin

Ingredients Use 1 poussin per person; a chicken will go further.
- 1 poussin per person
- Olive oil
- Sea salt & fresh ground black pepper
- Dried herbs or a marinade

Equipment
Chopping board, very sharp knife, barbecue

Spatchcocking is just a fancy word for flattening out a bird before cooking. I'm suggesting poussin, which is a young chicken – I do like the idea of everyone having a whole bird to eat to themselves.

A spatchcocked bird will cook over a grill in a fraction of the time it takes to roast a whole bird, which makes it perfect camping fodder. If you're able to light a real fire, you could even cook over the coals, à la Robin Hood and his Merry Men.

This dish goes really well with the feta, olive and red onion salad on p56 (which is, granted, slightly less Robin Hoodish).

To spatchcock the bird, place it on a chopping board breast-side up. Insert the knife into the body cavity and cut along the spine. You can then open out the bird ready for grilling.

Drizzle the poussin with olive oil, and then add a grind of pepper and a pinch of salt and sprinkle with dried herbs or brush with a marinade of your choice.

Grill the bird over a hot barbecue for 5 minutes or so on each side until it is cooked.

Drink suggestion A straightforward white – perhaps a Bordeaux Blanc, white Burgundy or Soave. Light reds, such as Beaujolais, and southern French reds from Minervois, Fitou or Corbières, would also go well. Avoid heavy reds.

Pan-braised game bird

Ingredients Serves 2

- A little olive oil
- 2 partridge or 4 quail (that's 1 partridge, or 2 quail, per person)
- 1 small onion, finely chopped
- 2 leeks, shredded and cut into 1cm lengths
- 1 dessertspoon plain flour
- Sea salt & fresh ground black pepper
- A large glass of white wine
- 500ml chicken stock (use a stock cube!)

Equipment

High-sided, non-stick frying pan – big enough to take two partridges – with a lid, sharp knife

I've always been a fan of game birds. As with the poussin (see p166), I like the idea of each person having one bird to themselves on a plate. Partridge are an ideal size for this, but you could use quail instead (in which case you'd probably need two each). Most good butchers will stock a range of game birds – though seasons vary by a few weeks depending on the bird, game is generally available from late autumn through to the spring.

Green beans with toasted sesame seeds (see p182) are a good side with this dish. The nutty flavour of the seeds does wonderful things with the woodsy taste of the bird.

Heat a little olive oil in a high-sided, non-stick frying pan and brown off the birds, then set aside on a plate.

Add a drop more oil to the pan and throw in the onion and leeks. Cook gently until the onions begin to colour, then add the flour, a pinch of sea salt and a good grind of black pepper and stir well. Add the wine a little at a time so the sauce doesn't go lumpy. Once all the wine is added, place the birds back in the pan – be sure to pour in any juices left on the plate.

Pour in the chicken stock around the birds and simmer very gently with the lid on the pan for 40 minutes. Remove the lid and simmer for another 5 minutes to thicken the cooking stock a little before serving.

Drink suggestion Pinot Noir goes well with game birds, but as this recipe uses white wine you could go for an unoaked Chardonnay from Burgundy or Australia, or a white from the South of France.

Chicken masala

A masala is simply a blend of spices, which can come in dry form or in a paste. At home, I would throw the spices in a blender with a small onion to bind them together, but in the field I take a different approach.

If you serve this with my perfect rice (see p96), a dollop of raita (p62) and warm pitta bread, I reckon that you could picture your tent pitched on the banks of the flowing Ganges – or at least on a rainy moor somewhere just outside Bradford, curry capital of Britain. Really, it tastes great wherever you eat it.

Mix the spices and the chopped chilli with the yogurt (this is the masala bit!) in a bowl, and add the chicken pieces. Give it a good stir to make sure all of the chicken is coated in the masala and let stand for at least 15 minutes.

In a high-sided, non-stick frying pan, heat the oil and cook the chopped onion until golden, then add the garlic and stir well. After a minute or so, add the chicken together with all the masala. Make sure the chicken seals on all sides.

If you are using fresh tomatoes, grate them into the pan, cut-side on the grater, leaving only the skin behind. Otherwise, just add your tin. Stir and allow to simmer for about half an hour. The sauce will thicken nicely as the moisture evaporates. If it gets a little too thick, just add a drop of water.

Sprinkle liberally with fresh chopped coriander and garnish with wedges of tomato just before serving.

Drink suggestion A cold lager always goes with a curry – Cobra if you can get it. Otherwise, try a Côtes de Gascogne wine.

Ingredients Serves 2

- ½ tsp ground cumin
- 1 tsp ground coriander
- 1 tsp paprika
- ½ tsp garam masala
- ¼ tsp turmeric
- 1 green chilli, de-seeded and finely chopped
- 3 tbsp plain yogurt
- 2 chicken breasts, cut into bite-sized chunks
- Olive oil
- 1 large onion, finely chopped
- 2 cloves of garlic, finely chopped
- 4 tomatoes, halved & grated (or you can use a tin of chopped toms if you like)
- A bunch of fresh coriander, chopped
- Tomato wedges

Equipment

Sharp knife, mixing bowl, high-sided, non-stick frying pan, grater (if using fresh tomatoes)

Quail à la Gordale

Ingredients Serves 2
- Olive oil
- 2 quail
- 1 red onion, chopped
- 1 clove of garlic, finely chopped
- ½ tsp bouillon powder
- Sea salt & fresh ground black pepper
- 1 sprig of fresh thyme
- 1 bay leaf
- 1 glass of red wine – a medium red is best, so as not to overwhelm the quail

Equipment
Small, heavy cast iron pot with tight-fitting lid, sharp knife

This dish is named after the campsite where I first prepared it – Gordale Scar in North Yorkshire. The idea, however, came from one of my favourite cookery writers, Elisabeth Luard, who includes a Bulgarian recipe for braised quail in her tome *European Peasant Cookery*. I messed around with it a little. Well, quite a lot really. This is actually nothing like the dish Luard describes! It's a superb camping supper, simple in its construction and smacking of the wild. Quail are small birds, so a hungry camper might eat two, but one each with a few vegetables or a hunk of crusty bread ought see off the hunger pangs for a while.

Brown the birds off in a good glug of hot olive oil in the bottom of a cast-iron pot. This adds flavour and improves the look of the final dish. Set the birds aside on a plate.

Add the chopped onion and garlic to the pot, letting them soften and colour gently. Cook for 4 or 5 minutes and, when the onions begin to take on a little colour, put the birds back in the pot along with the bouillon powder.

Season with sea salt and ground black pepper and add the fresh herbs. Pour in the glass of red wine. The liquid should half-cover the birds in the pan. You may need to add a drop of water.

Place the lid on the pot and allow to simmer very gently for 30 minutes.

Drink suggestion A Côtes du Rhône or a Beaujolais – especially a Morgon – or a Pinot Noir from the New World should all go well.

Valentine pork with caper sauce

I named this after Valentine Warner, after seeing him prepare it on one of his TV shows – I reckon it's got a better ring to it than "pork loin with caper and sage sauce". It's a fantastic dish, and one of my favourites. Ready in a matter of minutes, and packed full of strong, punchy flavours, it's good with a crunchy salad or boiled minted new potatoes and wilted spinach or Swiss chard.

Mix the flour with a generous grind of black pepper and a decent pinch of flaked sea salt. Coat the pork steaks on each side with the seasoned flour.

Heat some olive oil in a non-stick frying pan and fry the steaks for 2 or 3 minutes on each side.

While the pork is cooking, melt a generous knob of butter in a separate non-stick frying pan and add the chopped garlic and anchovy fillets. Throw in the capers and chopped sage leaves and give it a quick stir. The anchovies will have disintegrated by now (they're supposed to!).

Finally, squeeze in the lemon juice, give the sauce one last stir and spoon it over the steaks. Delicious!

Drink suggestion Such powerful flavours need a good but not overly fruity Sauvignon Blanc from France (Sancerre), Chile or South Africa. If you fancy a red, try a Chianti.

Ingredients Serves 4

- 1 tbsp plain flour
- Fresh ground black pepper
- Flaked sea salt
- 4 pork loin steaks
- Olive oil
- A large knob of butter
- 1 large clove of garlic, finely chopped
- 6 anchovy fillets
- 2 dessertspoons capers
- 8 fresh sage leaves, chopped
- Juice of a small lemon

Equipment

Two non-stick frying pans, sharp knife

Chicken fajitas

Ingredients Serves 4

- A couple of tbsp olive oil
- 1 medium onion, chopped
- 1 red pepper, thinly sliced
- 1 yellow pepper, thinly sliced (green will do if you can't find yellow)
- 2 cloves of garlic, finely chopped
- 2 chicken breasts, skin off
- ½ tsp paprika
- Sea salt & fresh ground black pepper
- 1 tin of chopped tomatoes
- A small bunch of fresh coriander, chopped (optional)
- 1 packet of flour tortillas (they usually come in packs of eight)
- 1 small tub of sour cream

Equipment
Sharp knife, high-sided frying pan, wooden spoon

Drink suggestion
Any crisp white or light red.

I owe this one to my daughter, who came home after having had her tea at a friend's house. "Daddy, Verity's mum cooked us chicken wraps for tea and I ate all of mine up!" That's my girl! Buzzing at the prospect of a whole new world of child-friendly cooking, I thought I'd recreate the dish on a trip to a tipi in Mid Wales. I whipped up a Mexican-style chicken wrap, packed with chilli and full of oomph – and watched my hopes crash as Ruby scraped out the chicken and simply ate the tortilla. Verity's mum 1, Guyrope Gourmet 0. Eventually I admitted defeat and opted to leave the chilli out altogether. This is the recipe that will see me equalise in the re-match!

Heat the olive oil in a large, high-sided, non-stick frying pan and add the finely chopped onion. Cook gently for 3 or 4 minutes and toss in the thinly sliced peppers.

Once the onion has begun to soften, add the finely chopped garlic and give it a quick stir. Cut the chicken breasts into chunks (2cm or so – not too big, as you need to be able to roll them up in the wraps) then add to the onion and garlic. Stir with a wooden spoon, making sure that the chicken is sealed on all sides.

Add the paprika, season with sea salt and ground black pepper and stir in the chopped tomatoes. Leave to simmer gently for 25 minutes; the sauce will begin to reduce and thicken. Remove from the heat and stir in the chopped fresh coriander, if you have it.

Place a couple of spoonfuls of the chicken and sauce on a flour tortilla, add a dollop of sour cream and get rolling!

Pheasant Vallée d'Auge

Ingredients Serves 2

- A big knob of butter
- 1 pheasant, jointed
- 300ml apple juice
- Bouquet garni
- Sea salt & fresh ground black pepper
- 1 tbsp cornflour
- 150ml double cream
- A handful of fresh flat leaf parsley, chopped

Equipment

A large saucepan

Submitted to the Guyrope Gourmet website by Mr Cripps of Wiltshire, this is an unbelievably easy variation on the classic French dish Poulet Vallée d'Auge, using apple juice in place of Calvados. It's included here on account of its simplicity – a spectacular, if a little posh-sounding, one pot wonder that's ideal for camping. If you don't fancy pheasant, or can't get hold of one out of season, you could always revert to the original recipe and use a chicken.

This is particularly delicious served with mashed potatoes and fried apple segments.

Heat the butter in a large saucepan and brown the jointed bird. Be careful not to burn the butter. Add the apple juice and bouquet garni, and add salt and pepper to taste. Bring to the boil, and then reduce the heat to a simmer.

After 10 minutes remove the bouquet garni and simmer for another 10 or 15 minutes.

Blend the cornflour into the double cream and add to the pan slowly, mixing thoroughly. Heat gently until the sauce thickens, and then throw in the chopped flat leaf parsley.

Drink suggestion A good Beaujolais or an off-dry white – a Pinot Gris from Alsace, perhaps. The apple juice will clash with dry whites or strong reds.

Tatws pum munud

This, a traditional Welsh dish of spuds and bacon in onion gravy, is an old family favourite; one of those recipes handed down from mother to son. I'll always associate my mother's cooking with tatws pum munud and the best homemade chips in the world. I used to eat this a lot when I was on the dole in the 1980s, serving my apprenticeship as the Giro Gourmet. For some reason my landlady, Gill, renamed it Tatty Bogals. I think she found it easier to pronounce.

Heat the olive oil in a high-sided, non-stick frying pan and cook the sliced onion for 2 or 3 minutes.

Trim the rashers of bacon into strips and add to the pan, together with the crumbled beef stock cube and the flour. Stir and cook for 1 minute. Add the sliced potatoes, season with salt and pepper and cook gently for another minute.

Add the water little by little, stirring all the while. Simmer gently until the potatoes are cooked through, adding more water if the gravy gets too thick.

Drink suggestion A light red wine goes nicely – as does a big mug of tea.

Ingredients Serves 4

- Olive oil
- 1 large onion, sliced
- 6 rashers of unsmoked back bacon
- 1 beef stock cube
- 1 dessertspoon plain flour
- 4 or 5 medium King Edward potatoes, peeled and sliced
- Sea salt & fresh ground black pepper
- 250ml water

Equipment

Sharp knife, large, high-sided, non-stick frying pan

Side dishes

THESE HUMBLE BUT DELICIOUS VEGETABLES, each given a simple embellishment, are all happy as Larry sitting beside a lovingly created main. The green beans with toasted sesame seeds are particularly good with salmon, while the wilted spinach is perfect with pork. As for the rosti, it's almost a disservice to call it a side dish. You could eat that as a meal in itself. Fresh vegetables will keep well in the camping larder, and the ones I've included here don't need to take up valuable room in the coolbox.

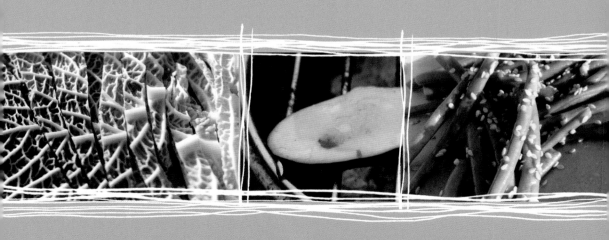

Wilted spinach and toasted garlic

Ingredients Serves 4

- A large bunch of fresh, young spinach
- 3 cloves of garlic
- Olive oil

Equipment

Kitchen paper, sharp knife, large frying pan, wooden spoon

This is an incredibly versatile side dish, working well with so many different things. It's great with fish and an absolute treat with grilled meats.

Wash the spinach and trim the stalks from the leaves. If you have large leaves, chop them roughly; if using the baby leaf variety, you can chuck them in whole. Pat the spinach dry after washing. It doesn't have to be bone dry, but too much water and it will end up soggy.

Peel and finely chop the garlic. Heat a glug of olive oil in a large frying pan. Throw in the garlic and stir, being very careful not to burn it. Keep the garlic moving in the pan until it just begins to turn golden.

Turn off the heat and add the spinach. Stir with a wooden spoon until the leaves begin to wilt. Serve hot!

Courgette "grillthings"

There's a made-up name if ever there was one! A made-up name for a stolen dish. The editor of *Lakeland Walker* magazine showed me how to make this while we were on a shoot for his mag. I love how the cheese melts and forms a tasty blanket over the basil leaf.

Slice the courgettes on the diagonal and drizzle with a little olive oil. Cook over the barbecue or on a hot griddle pan for about 3 minutes.

Turn the courgettes, place a single basil leaf and a sliver of cheese on the cooked side, and cook for a further 3 minutes. The cheese will melt over the basil leaf.

Season with ground black pepper.

Ingredients Serves 4
- 2 courgettes
- Olive oil
- A few fresh basil leaves
- A few shavings of Parmesan cheese
- Fresh ground black pepper

Equipment
A barbecue or a griddle pan

Green beans with toasted sesame seeds

Ingredients Serves 4

- 400g green beans
- A pinch of salt
- 1 tbsp sesame seeds
- A knob of butter

Equipment

Saucepan, small non-stick frying pan, sieve or colander

This side dish is a must with grilled fish. It came to me in a flash of inspiration while cooking for my pals on my 40th birthday. We were having grilled salmon, and I wanted a side dish that looked the business. The golden toasted seeds sticking to the verdant beans not only looked tempting but tasted superb – the nuttiness of the sesame works really well with the slight crunch of the beans. The only tricky bit is not burning the seeds!

Top and tail the beans and blanch in a saucepan of lightly salted boiling water for 5 minutes.

While the beans are cooking, lightly toast the sesame seeds in a dry non-stick frying pan over a moderate heat. Keep shaking the pan around to make sure the seeds don't stick. When they begin to take on a golden colour, they're ready.

Drain the beans well, throw them into a bowl, add the knob of butter and stir in the toasted seeds.

Savoy cabbage with mustard-seed butter

A simple vegetable to prepare and a splendid accompaniment to braised meats or filling stews, Savoy cabbages come into their prime in around November. This dish has the delicious air of autumn about it.

Shred the cabbage and steam it over boiling water – either in a steamer or in a colander with a lid, placed over a pan of water – until wilted but still a little al dente.

Meanwhile, melt the butter in the frying pan and gently fry the mustard seeds until they begin to crackle and pop.

Once the cabbage is cooked, drain it and turn it into a bowl. Pour the seeds and butter, along with a grind of black pepper, over the cabbage. Turn with a fork and serve.

Ingredients Serves 4
- ○ 1 small Savoy cabbage (outer leaves removed)
- ○ A knob of butter
- ○ 1 tbsp mustard seeds
- ○ A grind of fresh black pepper

Equipment
Sharp knife, bamboo vegetable steamer (or colander, lid and pan), small frying pan, bowl

Rosti with halloumi

Ingredients Serves 4

- 500g waxy potatoes (Charlottes are good)
- 1 small onion
- 100g halloumi
- 1 sprig of fresh rosemary
- Fresh ground black pepper
- Olive oil

Equipment

Saucepan, large bowl, grater, sharp knife, non-stick frying pan, wooden spoon

I tip a thankful nod in the direction of Deri Reed, the Ethical Chef, for this one. Watching him cook it at the Really Wild Food Festival in St Davids, the thing that really caught my eye was that he added halloumi. The cheese lends it a moreish, sticky texture, and gives a Cypriot twist to the traditional Swiss breakfast dish. This is my approximation of Deri's creation, based on having watched him cook it once. I dare say that he would do a better job!

You don't need to add salt to this dish; the halloumi has enough salt of its own.

Parboil the potatoes whole, with the skin on, in a saucepan of boiling water for 4 minutes. Remove from the heat, drain and top up the pan with cold water to stop the cooking process. Drain the potatoes and allow them to cool.

Once they're cool enough to handle, grate the potatoes into a large bowl, using the coarse side of the grater. Don't worry about the skin – most of it will end up in your hand after grating. Next, grate in the onion and the halloumi.

Finely chop the rosemary leaves and add them to the bowl along with a good grind of black pepper. Mix it all together thoroughly with your fingertips. (It gets a bit sticky, so have a cloth to hand!)

You can either make individual rostis or cook the whole lot together in one and cut it up later – it's really up to you.

Either way, heat a little olive oil in a non-stick frying pan. Add the rosti. If you're making one big one, spread the mixture evenly over the bottom of the pan. If you're making individual portions, use a small handful per portion. Squash the mixture flat with the back of a wooden spoon and cook it gently for about 4 minutes.

Flip the rosti in the pan by tipping it onto an oiled plate and then slipping it back into the hot pan, uncooked side down. Cook for a further 4 minutes to brown off.

Sautéed courgettes with mint

Ingredients Serves 2

- A knob of butter
- 3 or 4 courgettes, sliced at an angle
- 6 or 8 fresh mint leaves, finely chopped
- Lots of fresh ground black pepper
- A tiny pinch of sea salt

Equipment

Sharp knife, non-stick frying pan

This was a try-it-and-see attempt to get my children to eat courgettes. It worked. I think they were confused by the addition of mint and by the fact that I called the courgette by its American name, zucchini!

It's an unusual combo, with the zippy fragrance of the mint cutting through the buttery courgettes. You could also use this as a pasta topping, scattered with Parmesan shavings.

Heat the butter in a non-stick frying pan and sauté the sliced courgettes until they take on a little colour.

Add the finely chopped mint leaves, a really good grind of black pepper and a little salt. Toss in the pan and serve.

INNOVATIVE
FAMILY CAMPING

INVEST IN THE BEST

UNFORGETTABLE MOMENTS

We believe in quality time camping with family and friends

INNOVATION AND DESIGN

We create market-leading, award-winning tents and equipment so you can safely and comfortably camp in all weathers

FACEBOOK

Share the Outwell camping experience with our lively community

Index

Acknowledgements

I've been using Outwell kit for many years now. It's reliable and does what it sets out to do. In recent years, and particularly during the production of this book, Outwell have kindly sponsored the Guyrope Gourmet by supplying me with a wide range of equipment, from tents to teapots – and I've come to see the tent that I use for my cookery demonstrations, an Outwell Monterey 5, as my second home. A good manufacturer will listen to their customers and be willing to adapt their products accordingly. Outwell certainly do a lot of that, and I commend them for it. I'd like to take this opportunity to thank Outwell and the team at Oase Outdoors for their enthusiastic support.

I have many other people I wish to thank.
Anne-Marie, Ruby and Wilf, who make camping fun. My father, Alan, who among many other things, taught me the importance of folding a groundsheet properly. My step-mum Jude, who taught me the rudiments of cooking. Mr. "Tank" Cripps, who first introduced me to the Trangia stove. Nick Harper, Glyn Smyth and Rob Little for listening and encouraging. Trevor and Lisa for the first Guyrope Gourmet website and logo. Fal for a later website and loads of other design work. James Stark for his drinks suggestions. Mark Sutcliffe for giving me a leg-up when I was starting out as a freelance writer. Iain Duff for giving me regular work. Tim Hayward and Kate Hawkings for helping me find more work. Joan Ransley for introducing me to the Guild of Food Writers. John, Costa and Jane at The Cove in Otley for teaching me a thing or two about cooking for the great British public.

A big thanks to all the people who have looked at my website, followed me on Twitter, and those who come and say hello when I'm doing a show.

A special thanks to Clive Garrett and Jonathan Knight, who brought the book to fruition, and to editor Samantha Cook and designer Diana Jarvis who, between them, shaped and crafted my words and pictures to deliver a book beyond my dreams.

Thanks, also, to those who submitted recipes via the Guyrope Gourmet website
Rob Little, James Stark, Moose Harris, Sue (@gardinerbyname), Alan Harrison (@chalkypilot).

Credits

Editor
Samantha Cook

Design and additional photography
Diana Jarvis

Illustrations
Josh Sutton, Ruby Sutton

Front cover photo
Andy Bulmer

Additional photo credits
Diana Jarvis, Steve Cripps, Anne-Marie Davies, Frances Dyson Sutton, Alan Sutton, Vikki Woodward, Max Thornton, Mark Sutcliffe, Marie Ayres, Andy Bulmer

Proofreader
Leanne Bryan

Publisher
Jonathan Knight